By the same author

BRAVE MEN CHOOSE
JOHN WESLEY, ANGLICAN
GOOD GOD IT WORKS!
REBIRTH OF A NATION?
STRANGELY WARMED
GOD'S POLITICIAN: WILLIAM WILBERFORCE'S STRUGGLE
FRANK BUCHMAN: A LIFE

With Sir Arnold Lunn

THE NEW MORALITY
THE CULT OF SOFTNESS
CHRISTIAN COUNTER-ATTACK

With Sydney Cook

THE BLACK AND WHITE BOOK

The above books and most of the others mentioned in this book can be obtained from Grosvenor Books.

CAST OUT YOUR NETS

Sharing your Faith with others

GARTH LEAN

GROSVENOR
LONDON · MELBOURNE · WELLINGTON
OTTAWA · RICHMOND VA

First published 1990
GROSVENOR BOOKS
54 Lyford Road, London, SW18 3JJ

21 Dorcas Street, South Melbourne
Victoria 3205, Australia

Suite 405, 251 Bank Street
Ottawa, Ontario K2P 2HI
Canada

PO Box 1834, Wellington,
New Zealand.

GROSVENOR USA
PO Box 8647
Richmond, VA 23226

© 1990 Garth Lean

British Library Cataloguing in Publication Data
Lean, Garth
Cast out your nets
1. Personal evangelism
Counselling. Autobiography
I. Title
248.5
ISBN 1–85239–010–7

Design: Blair Cummock
Cover: Cameron–Johnson

Phototypeset in Palatino by Input Typesetting Ltd, London
Printed and bound by Biddles of Guildford, England.

CONTENTS

	Introduction	1
1	Knowing Yourself	7
2	Winning Trust	19
3	Listening	25
4	Honesty Begets Honesty	37
5	Confession – Why? How?	47
6	Willing to Warn	53
7	Facing the Truth	61
8	Decision	73
9	Putting Things Right	85
10	Follow Through	93
11	Growth	101
12	Families	111
13	Three Levels of Life	115
14	Building a Team	121
15	Your Major Passion	129
	Epilogue	133

TO MARGOT,
the bravest of the brave,
for waiting ten years for me
and for forty-four wonderful years
together – and more to come

INTRODUCTION

Young friends of mine have told me recently that they know many sincere Christians of their own age who feel puzzled about how to help their friends – especially those who are agnostic or atheist – to find a living faith.

Indeed, the puzzle is not confined to the young. A large number of older people have, from time to time, told me the same thing. Many seem to have come to the point of thinking it an impossible task. I remember suggesting to one gifted politician, a convinced Christian, that he might try and help a colleague who was obviously in deep water. "I could not possibly," he replied. I asked him if he would seek God's will to see whether there was anything in the idea, but he would not consider it. Whether he was uncertain what he could or would say, whether fear entered in or whether he thought any such intervention would be interpreted as an intrusion into his colleague's privacy, I do not know. I could understand any of these reactions, because I have often felt them myself when faced with a need in one of my friends. But, so often, when I have dared to speak, the other person has been grateful and met me halfway.

One individual helping another towards faith is now perhaps the most neglected of all the ways which Jesus himself used and of which he left us many examples.

While moving house recently, I came across the following manuscript, which was written during World War II, on a Suffolk farm. In it I tried to summarise what I had learnt about "fishing for people" in the ten years since I had been, quite unexpectedly, "fished" myself by the Oxford Group during my fourth term at university. The Oxford Group in the twenties and thirties was a kind of spiritual explosion which gave dozens of undergraduates and some dons an initial or deeper experience of Christ and trained them to become fishers of people. This led to what the then unregenerate Malcolm Muggeridge described as "the only" religious awakening to come out of Britain in that decade.[3]

Talking to my young friends last year, it occurred to me that my long-neglected manuscript might be of some help to them, as well as to some older Christians, and so I now publish it. I have left it as originally written, only slightly edited for clarity and nowhere updated, except by a few contemporary footnotes and one passage (printed in italics), which seemed to illustrate some point usefully.

When I wrote this manuscript I had not met many

---

[1] I had been classified unfit for military service
[2] Cf Matthew 4:19
[3] Malcolm Muggeridge, *The Thirties*, (Hamish Hamilton, 1940) p. 20

Roman Catholics – still less people of other religions – from all of whom I have since learnt much. The Catholics whom I did meet and who showed interest, I counselled to see their priests. (I should also mention that my references are incomplete, as I cannot always remember what versions of the Bible or which biographies of St. Francis or Wesley I was then quoting.)

I was not attempting to set down any technique – for there is no human technique whereby peoples' lives can be transformed. Only God can change people. Yet it would seem that he sometimes uses, and even needs, human instruments. After all, Jesus called his first disciples with the promise that he would "make them fishers of men"[1] an active pursuit. He sent them out in pairs to do it and "thrilled" at their reports on their return. When he saw Peter after the Resurrection, he three times told him to care for his "sheep" and "lambs", and his last instruction to his followers at the Ascension was that they should "go and make disciples in all nations". He also promised them the gift of the Holy Spirit to direct their actions and lead them into all truth.

The attempt to win individuals has obvious dangers. Ambition can enter in and lead to head-hunting and pride. But, the Holy Spirit will provide correctives, either directly or through those with whom we

---

[1] Greek scholars tell me that the word used for men in Matthew 4:19 applies to both men and women. An accurate translation might be "From now on you will be fishermen capturing people."

are working, if we keep open to them. Surely it is even more dangerous not to try, or to be so fearful or tentative in our approaches that people are not stimulated to consider a real change taking place within them? After all, the aim of "life-changing", as the Oxford Group often called "fishing for people", is not to compel or dominate anyone, but to free them and offer them a stimulus to discover for themselves God's fullest idea of what he or she can be. It is the art of unfolding the possibilities there are in people and offering them that transforming friendship with God which Jesus promised.

Most of us in the period covered by this book acted with this belief. Something wonderful had happened to us. It was natural to tell others about it, out of gratitude for God's forgiveness. Often friends did not need to be told. They saw we were different. When Margot Appleyard, my wife-to-be, decided one evening in November 1932 at Somerville College to give her life to God, three of her friends approached her in the next three days and asked her what had happened to her. She told them. All three responded by telling her of grave troubles in themselves and their families – which they had not mentioned before – and decided at once to make the same experiment which Margot had made. Each of them found new freedom and reported, after the following vacation, that this had notably affected their situations.

A Russian professor, speaking at a conference in

[1] We did not marry until 1946, after this manuscript was written.

Introduction

Switzerland in 1989, told of finding the same freedom. It was his "greatest experience". "It happened in three stages," he said. "Firstly a freedom from the yoke of the state which stops you thinking your thoughts. Then there was the discovery of God, of an inner freedom, of a world full of the unexpected, the miraculous, of divine love for each individual. "Finally, I've learnt here something for my life: that inner freedom can't just be our private property. We must share it, and refuse the privilege of being free, alongside others who are not free."

In this manuscript, I wrote the chapters in an order which outlines stages through which a person often goes in the search for a faith. I did not mean that this was the only way people could come to God, for he obviously reaches them through many ways and uses countless other people and agencies. Nor did I see these chapters as a series of hoops through which everyone must pass. Rather they contain experiences through which a "fisher of people" as well as those he or she helps, will pass at some time – indeed many times – along the way. They are simply discoveries that I personally made when I, the most Incompleat of Anglers, went a-fishing.

Garth Lean,
Oxford, May 1990

Chapter One

KNOWING YOURSELF

The experience of finding a faith has been summed up in three sentences: "The disease is sin. Christ is the cure. The result is a miracle." To know yourself accurately, you must understand sin. Many, of course, have abolished it – on paper. Using their minds to kill their consciences, they maintain that self-indulgence is natural, or that it is the inevitable result of an unjust society. They seem to think a problem ignored or explained is a problem cured. Alas, it is not so. You can demonstrate that cancer is the natural result of certain causes, but that is chill comfort to the man who dies of it.

It may be said that the commonest kinds of sin come from the perversion of our strongest instincts – the urges to recreate the species, to keep body and soul together and to make one's way in the world. Sex, money, career. But the list is far from exhaustive. More immediately helpful is this simple working definition: "Sin is anything that gets between you and God or between you and another person."

But how to understand and begin to cure a disease with so many forms?

"Know yourself," said Socrates to his disciple

Plato. "Be ye perfect," added Jesus to his disciples.[1] In that battle within, insight and understanding are born. Of Jesus himself it was said: "He knew all men and required no evidence from anyone about human nature."[2] Was it not in part because he was "in all points tempted like as we are, yet without sin"?[3]

I first began really to know myself when I was forced by several failures to face that I needed to become different. The two principal stimulants were the arrival of the Northern Hunger Marchers in Oxford en route for London and my relationship with a certain girl.

I felt guilty at having it so good at university, while the unemployed – then three million of them dependent on a means-tested dole of ten shillings a week – were having it so bad. I dared not go and see them because I knew that my life, as I was planning it, would contribute nothing to them or to anyone else. I felt I needed a new, unselfish purpose for which to live.

With the girl it was much the same. She had told me she loved me. I did not love her, but let the relationship go along for what I could get out of it. It suddenly struck me that I was being as unfair to her as the nation was being to the unemployed.

Very reluctantly I asked a man in college called Kit Prescott whether we could have a talk. I had been

---

[1] Matthew 5:48
[2] John 2:25
[3] Hebrews 4:15

Knowing Yourself

avoiding him ever since he had remarked some months before that God had a plan for my life.

We had tea in his digs, and, for the first time in my life, I was honest with someone about my hopes and ambitions, my fears and my failures. "What is this plan which God has for me?" I asked.

"I don't know," he replied, "but God will tell you if you ask him, ready to obey."

He said it would mean giving my life to God, and that would entail facing Christ's moral standards. These, he summed up as absolute honesty, purity, unselfishness and love.[1] "Absolute?" said I. "Yes," he replied. "Otherwise you'll let yourself off with relative standards, and end by staying as you are and saying, 'I'm no saint, but I am a lot better than X or Y or Z.'" I realised that this had been exactly my attitude.

Silence fell between us, and ways in which I had cheated two of my brothers immediately popped into

---

[1]These four absolutes were first used as a summary of Christ's moral teaching by Robert E. Speer, after whom a library in Princeton University is named, in his *Principles of Christ* (Fleming Revell, 1902). They were standards anyone, however simple or scholarly, could use to measure his life, and the added prefix, "absolute", while setting an aim no one could attain, had two obvious advantages. It stopped the honest seeker from letting himself off with a second or third best or by the relativism which adjusts to the society around him; and it set so high a goal that anyone attempting to live by the standards would constantly be forced back to God for forgiveness, grace and strength. These standards do not impose any hard and fast rules. They are interpreted to each person by the Holy Spirit according to what that person is ready for at each period.

my mind. Before we parted, as I will describe more fully later, I had decided to put these things right, and, as an experiment, to give my life to God and see whether he would give me the strength to live a new way.

Kit also suggested that I should, each morning before breakfast, give a quarter of an hour to listen to God, ready to receive both correction and direction from him.

Certainly it was with the small beginnings of battling with my own faults that the first rays of understanding about others came into my self-centred mind. And I have found this: although through the luck of upbringing and circumstances I had never done the more violent sins which society punishes, yet during hundreds of honest talks in the last ten years I have never met anyone whose problems I could not understand from knowing my own temptations.

Chesterton's Father Brown, who solved many crimes but always put the winning of the criminal's soul first, once said: "The more you learn about yourself, the more you understand other people, and the more you learn about other people, the more you understand yourself."

How much alike we all are. I realised this simple, far-reaching truth the day I met my first burglar. It was at a West Country vicarage. The meeting, it is only fair to add, was by arrangement and in daylight. All the same the good lady of the house took the precaution of locking the dining-room door, where

Knowing Yourself

her silver was. What she did not know was that Tommy and I were already inside.

There we were. I was nineteen years old, on my first life-changing excursion outside the university. I had lived a sheltered kind of life, and a few months ago considered myself an agnostic. Tommy was forty-five, a tough old lag of four convictions. He was married and had several children. He still thieved for a living, if lately on a less grand scale. What had we in common? I was far more afraid of having no message for him than that he would pinch the silver.

All I could do was to tell Tommy about my recent change. In particular, I described how that decision turned at one point on being honest with one of my brothers. I had had to admit that I used to sneak up to his room and read his private correspondence. I had done it once. I had done it again. And, once, I had stolen money from another brother's drawer. I could not seem to stop, though I knew it was mean. It fascinated me.

Now it was Tommy who was fascinated. He was gazing back at me with understanding in his eyes. His first job, said he, had been plundering mail bags. How did I manage to stop?

A remarkable coincidence? No. For as we went through the standards of absolute honesty, purity, unselfishness and love together, we found many other failures in common. Often he had done the thing I had longed to do in the secret places of my heart. I had thought; he had acted. Christ did not rate the wrong thought indulged as any better than the wrong deed.[1] We were a pair. Beginning to know myself, I could understand him.

How Tommy ended up, I don't know. I had not then learnt to keep in touch with people. Later that evening when I told my host, the vicar, of my discovery, he said: "Never think, Garth, that a collar turned round, or even a pair of gaiters, makes any difference to temptation. You and Tommy and I – we are a trio."

* * * * * *

I found another thing. If there is any known temptation in my life which I am not fighting, I am unlikely to notice or take up that fault clear-sightedly in others. Where I am soft on myself I will be soft on others. That is a part of the protective mechanism which we all have inside us. "Lest at any time they should see with their eyes, and hear with their ears, and should understand with their heart, and should be converted, and I should heal them."[2]

I remember once early on a friend of mine was getting entangled in a relationship with a girl who was hindering him in his search for God. At the time I was myself keener on planning a future marriage for myself than doing God's will – and I had not even noticed what was happening. A more experienced friend arrived at that moment and took in the

[1] Matthew 5:21–30
[2] Matthew 13:15

Knowing Yourself 13

situation at a glance. He said nothing to my friend. He turned to me and said, "Garth, when are you going to make up your mind to deal with yourself?"

I was blind to my friend's danger because I was flirting with a similar danger myself. No one is so blind as the man who does not want to see.

* * * * * *

The most important discovery of my second year at university, however, was that God could tell me not only about my own needs but about other people's too, if I listened to him in the right spirit.

Up to then I had been totally baffled if friends came to me with their worries. Sometimes I would roll off a gramophone-like record of the rules of spiritual health – which I knew, and they sensed, I did not practise myself. Sometimes I simply said, "You must cut it out, old man," without giving any idea how it could be done. Most often I took the even easier road, "Yes, it's rotten luck. Let's go to the flicks and forget about it." I had no idea what was behind their worries, what was the real solution to them.

So when in my second year I set out on my earliest life-changing adventures, I put my difficulty to Prescott. "God will tell you people's needs, if you love them enough and pray for them disinterestedly and persistently," he replied. "He told me yours, you know." And out of his pocket he drew the notebook in which, morning by morning, he wrote down the thoughts which came as he opened his heart and mind to God. There, among the thoughts Prescott had written down for the day on which I approached him and asked his help, were these words: "Pray for Lean. Cancel your afternoon plan. He will want to spend it with you." And there, also in black and white, was the description of my most stubborn problem of those days, which I had never mentioned to Kit or to anyone else in the university.

I was amazed. Yet today it seems normal enough. For I know by repeated experience that if you pray for someone with love in your heart, think of him with whatever power you have and ask God for guidance about him, the insight will often be given you. It may take time, but the growing sense of certainty or the sudden illuminating flash will often come. You will be told how best to help: whether you should take any action, or just wait.

* * * * * *

So two fundamentals of spiritual insight are to listen to God and daily to wrestle with our own temptations. They are the essentials. With these principles firmly established in mind and practice, there are many useful aids.

You can learn from a person's habits and mannerisms, from his taste in literature, his turns of phrase, his way of dressing, his vehemences and his silences. Experience, and study of your own reactions, will show you how to interpret the signs of need.

Sometimes a person will attack most violently that

Knowing Yourself

part of Christ's challenge and message of which he stands in greatest need. Sometimes, again, the talkative will fall silent when the conversation nears a tender spot. Or the silent will try desperately to change the subject.

This is not the place to chronicle all the signs. There are many other books which do it far better and more fully than I can. And better still, there are men and women in need on every hand. Read many people rather than many books. If your eye is single, and you are honest with yourself, you will often see how you can help. In God's mind everyone has a next step, no matter how self-assured he or she seems or how much more Christ-like he or she is than you or I. It is always possible that God might wish to reveal that next step through you.

* * * * * *

What I meant by "guidance" and "listening to God" is assumed in the original narrative, but not explained until much later in the book. It was the kind of two-way prayer practised by prophets in the Bible and by many saints down the ages. Thus, Isaiah wrote: "Morning by morning he wakens my ear to hear as those who are taught."[1] And St. Augustine prayed, "Often I heard you teaching and commanding. It is my delight, in which I take refuge whenever I can relax from the duties laid upon me."[2] St. Francis

---

[1] Isaiah 50:4, Revised Standard Version
[2] *Confessions*, Book 10, XL, 65

de Sales, in An Introduction to the Devout Life, *wrote of such listening, "Engage in this spiritual exercise an hour every day before the main, midday meal, early in the morning if possible, because then your mind will be less distracted and more fresh after the repose of the night."*[1]

Prescott told me, as indeed St. Francis implies, that ordinary people can and should so listen, and that thoughts would come from God if one was ready to obey. Among those who influenced me at the time was the distinguished New Testament scholar, B.H. Streeter, when he wrote in The God Who Speaks: *"It would seem then to accord with Christ's teaching that, whenever possible, we should begin the day by attuning the soul to the contemplation of the Divine (by some act of aspiration or by reading scripture or other noble words) and should then, before offering petitions of personal needs, wait in silence – listening, if haply the inner voice should bring some guidance, some indication of the part in God's plan which the worshipper may be called upon to play that day. Often to those who listen so there comes a thought or word, clear and definite, pointing to action. But if no such come, it matters little. The mind has been attuned to the divine, and therefore is more likely to react aright to the situations, unexpected and unforeseen, which every day brings forth."*[2]

No one believed that every thought which passed through his mind at such a time of listening came from God, but,

---

[1] p.64, Hodder and Stoughton, edited by Peter Toon.
[2] *The God Who Speaks*, (Macmillan, 1936), being a revision of his Warburton Lectures 1933–35, pp. 27–28.

unfortunately, some of us used the word "guidance" loosely at times, giving this false impression.

Chapter Two
WINNING TRUST

It is said that Nelson could not have won the Battle of Copenhagen, his "masterpiece", without the help of a turbot. It was a huge fish which one of his officers caught and presented to him. He sent it through heavy seas to his commander-in-chief, Admiral Sir Hyde Parker.

That comfort-loving, indecisive aristocrat distrusted his upstart second-in-command, who had recently been ennobled after his destruction of Napoleon's fleet at the Battle of the Nile. Parker had made up his mind to have as little as possible to do with him, had not told him of his orders or plans and had steadily ignored the memoranda which Nelson sent him. Indeed, when diplomacy failed, Parker wanted to retire to England. Nelson, knowing that the Russians had just joined the Danes and Swedes on Napoleon's side and that, if they got together, Britain would be faced with a hostile fleet of 120 ships of the line in the Baltic, felt it essential to eliminate the Danish fleet.

Luckily Parker liked fish, and it was thought that the turbot "broke the ice between the two men". A little rhyme went round the fleet as it lay indecisive in the Kattegat:

> "Nelson's prepared to grow thinner
> And give Parker a turbot bright,
> If Parker will only eat dinner
> And let Lord Nelson fight."

Nelson was thereafter called into conference, and in the end was given command of the independent squadron with which he sailed to victory. The turbot may have done more than argument or memoranda in winning Parker's trust.

To win the other person's trust is the first job with anyone we want to help. Yet many Christians, in common with other folk, neglect this vital element in human relationships. They seem to think that if, from pulpit or chair, they say the true thing theologically and point out the right course, their duty is fulfilled.

It is rather like the recruit at the shooting range. He was obviously enjoying himself hugely. When asked whether he was hitting the target, he beamed: "I don't know that, sergeant; but they sure leave here with the hell-of-a-bang."

The recruit was not interested in the receiving end. The same is true of very many of us. Yet the receiving end is what matters. We will never help another to change his way of living unless we are chiefly interested in what is going on inside him, and what his aims are.

In proposing change to people we are really suggesting that they risk present reputation and future prospects, that they bet their lives on the existence

Winning Trust

of a God of love and power. People do not bet money, let alone life and future, on the say-so of someone they do not trust.

So, though we have a real insight into a person's problems, and moreover the answer for them in our own experience plus a God-given vision for his or her future, our first task must be to win his or her trust. Without that we will be helpless.

All of us know the relief of talking deeply, without reserve, to a chosen friend. They are the times one remembers undimmed through the years, and to many they come so seldom that they stand out in memory associated with only one or two people, or even with certain rare occasions with those people. Here is a person to whom we can tell all our hopes and fears and loves and ambitions, our defeats as well as our victories. Here is someone from whom we will take the truth, even if it is unpleasant, because there is friendship between us. By his loyalty he had earned the right to speak, and we have the same freedom with him.

It is the life-changer's privilege and vocation to work for such a mature relationship with each person he meets. But there is this difference. The relationship will not be just for its own sake, but for God's sake. And so it must be bracing, purposeful. It must be less sentimental than that of the mythical policeman who found a man about to jump off Westminster Bridge into the Thames. It is said that he induced the fellow to desist on the understanding that they would talk the matter over – but that ten minutes later they both jumped in. Which is very much what used to happen with me in my first year at the university when, over coffee and a fire, my college cronies came to discuss life with me.

* * * * * *

How can mature friendship be built, and built swiftly, with people whom we have never met before and with whom we may have little in common?

I remember well a bleak December day in New York, when the wind was shrieking round the Flatiron Building. A friend came into the house where some of us were staying and said that George Macdonald wanted to see us at his hotel.

The anouncement was unexpected. Macdonald (I have changed his name) was a politician. He had gained fame in his recent whirlwind but unsuccessful campaign to stop President Roosevelt's return to the White House. He had spoken to several million people, and his tongue had been so bitter that the newspapers had christened him "Rabble-Rouser Number One".

We sat down and listened to God together, asking him who should go and see him. The task fell to three of us. All of us admitted that Macdonald's name conjured up an unpleasant picture. For one of us was a strong Roosevelt man, while another, though opposed to Roosevelt politically, shied away from Macdonald's flamboyant methods. Being English I was neutral, but all three of us had seen a

Winning Trust

hostile news film about the man which had, as its makers intended, nauseated us.

The idea that came to us all was simple but fundamental. "Love Macdonald for his own sake. Don't argue, but listen. Keep to the point of change. Don't be tempted to argue on smaller points of view." We prayed for that love as we set out to meet him.

Macdonald met us at the door of his suite. He smiled warmly, shook hands firmly. But as we passed into the room, he shot a quick glance down the passage to make sure that no-one was lurking there to apply his ear to the key-hole. For, rightly or wrongly, Macdonald felt himself a hunted man. He was convinced that his closest friend and political associate had been murdered on orders from Washington and that he himself was being followed.

We sat down and Macdonald began to talk. He was watching us for reactions with the intensity of a sensitive man who has hurt many – and been much hurt.

We listened. Presently he became provocative. He stated his political views with force. He abused the President and others of his enemies. We continued to listen. One, two, three hours passed, and none of us had said more than a few sentences.

Gradually Macdonald's protective armour slid away. He told us with emotion about his family, his wife and his boy at college. He described vividly and with humour how he had been "omeletted" by a shower of bad eggs at a recent meeting.

At midnight, after we had been with him four

hours, he saw us on our way to the subway. "My," he said, "this evening has done me good. I can talk to you fellows. You're disinterested somehow. Next time, *I'll* listen."

We met many times that month. On Christmas Eve we saw him off from Grand Central Station to spend the holiday with his boy. On his way to the station, he posted a letter to the President, apologising for the hatred he had brought into their political differences. What the letter did not say was that Macdonald had that week rejected a seven figure sum, offered him on condition he took part in a dishonest campaign against the President.

Much in Macdonald's life became different. Much, perhaps, still needed to change. But that is another story. The point of the tale is that his trust was won and that, after a month, he was doing some things because God ordered them, which no amount of human argument, threat or persuasion would have compelled him to do.

Chapter Three
LISTENING

"God gave a man two ears and one mouth", goes the old saying, "Why don't you listen twice as much as you talk?" To listen to God and to listen to the other person are two of the profoundest secrets of life-changing. And how difficult we self-absorbed people find it. We talk of having to suffer bores gladly. We might well remember the definition of a bore – someone who talks about himself when you want to talk about yourself. It is amazing how interesting people can be when you deliberately give up the luxury of talking yourself.

The need to be free from the domination of your opinions and prejudices is almost as important. It is not a question of having no opinions. But it does mean seeing that they can be out of place when you are trying to win a person's trust. There will be plenty of time to talk about them later.

Points of view are the reason why so many people clash on superficial levels and fail to help people to change on the fundamental moral and spiritual level. Macdonald, by his abuse, was tempting us to disagree politically. But the point of view may equally well be theological or social, professional or economic. And it is our "good" points of view that are the most dangerous – for there we are so sure that we are right.

St. Peter, for instance, grew up with the conviction that it was wrong to eat certain things or to eat with Gentiles. That principle could have confined him too narrowly, but for God's intervention on the Joppa roof exactly as Cornelius' messengers approached his door. And Peter's first reaction to God is interesting, because timeless. "No, no, Lord. I have never eaten anything common or unclean." He was given grace to see the wider vision.[1] Think what Cornelius and his waiting friends – and the world – would have missed had he stuck to his traditional idea. "I am made all things to all men that I might by all means save some," said St. Paul.[2]

Perhaps these two gifts from God – the deliverance from the itch to talk and from the lust to clash on minor matters – were some of the substance of the "disinterestedness" which Macdonald felt. The positive side, the other face of the penny, was that we were given a real affection for him as a person. Such an affection cannot be faked. A person instantly senses if it is just a spiritual bedside manner, assumed for the moment, to be shed outside the door. He feels he is being manipulated, that you are being professional or have an axe to grind. And nothing so destroys friendship. No one likes to be "reformed" for some ulterior motive of the reformer

[1] Acts 10
[2] I Corinthians 19:22

Listening

– whether it is that the change would make the reformer's life easier (how many parents treat their children thus!) or that it would fit in with his theory or give him a warm sense of achievement.

Henry Drummond's[1] biographer describes his view of this as one of his fellow students. He was at Edinburgh University when Drummond returned from his first great mission, a famous man, at the age of 23. "We were a little afraid of him and his chances for tackling us", he writes. "But we felt he was interested in us, and his interest being without officiousness won our confidence and made us frank with him. We could tell him, as we could not tell others, the worst about ourselves – the worst, and, just as easily also, the best – our ideals and ambitions, of which men are often as ashamed to speak as of their sins. To the latter he was never indulgent, or aught but faithful. But in every man he saw good, which the man himself had forgotten or was ignorant of."[2]

That is the sense you have with every genuine life-changer. You feel the warmth of his love – he loves you for your own sake. You know that he has vision and faith for your future. You know he would like you to march along with him. And yet, there is complete independence. Almost a nonchalance. He will never let you down. And he will never let you off. Yet whatever you do, he is going on and will remain

---

[1] Geologist and evangelist, author of *Natural Law in the Spiritual World*.
[2] *Life of Henry Drummond* by George Adam Smith, p. 106–107

your friend. The decision is left to you. You can take it or leave it.

This "independence" – which is really just loyalty to God – must be central. There is a wrong-headed notion among many Christians that the way to win people's confidence is to lower your standards until you are as much like them as possible. But what is the result if you do? They may feel comfortable with you, and you will avoid persecution. But no one will be changed at all fundamentally.

I am reminded of the true story of my friend Charlie and the psycho-analyst.

When the scene opens, Charlie, a first world war pilot, had lost career and wife and family through complete inability to keep off the bottle.

When all else had failed, Charlie's friends persuaded him to visit a psycho-analyst. She cross-examined Charlie closely. She delved deftly into his past. She searched his present. The session lasted till seven o'clock when Charlie suggested they adjourn for dinner. They repaired to one of Charlie's nicer speak-easies. To be polite, and study him the better, she drank with him glass for glass. When they parted some hours later the commissionaire packed each into a separate taxi. It was hard to tell doctor from patient.

Two years later, Charlie met a man who told him simply that since drink was a problem for him he would have to cut it out. The man had never been a heavy drinker himself, and now drank no alcohol. But he had had his own stubborn problems – and

Listening

was now victorious over them. He assured Charlie that, if he really wished it, God could give him the power to make a clean break. Charlie was fascinated by the fellow. He was so *different*.[1] Soon Charlie decided to make the experiment. Today he is reunited with his wife and out of debt, the father of a happy family.

No. People do not want you to be *like* them. Their imagination will never be caught by a "moderate" version of themselves. There is no point in their leaving cherished plans or much-loved indulgences to be that. They want freedom, the assurance in your life and bearing that real victory is available. So never put down the hurdles. Help your friend tackle them at their full height in a strength greater than his own.

The decision to change is finally, as we shall see, an act of the will. But often one needs to fire a person's imagination in some way first. Most people start out with the idea that human nature cannot be changed, least of all their own. If you ask them outright to make a decision to give their lives to God without first showing them what it can mean to themselves and to others, even to their country, their answer is quite likely to be like that of an East London woman of whom a surgeon friend of mine asked permission to perform a necessary operation. "It is all very well

---

[1] Professor William Barclay wrote that the word St. Paul used when he wrote to "the saints" in various towns simply means "those who are different".

for you to ask permission," she replied, "but who will pay for the funeral?"

People's first thought about changing is often that they will have to give something up. They may be right – but it is nothing in comparison with what they will receive. Jesus promised, "There is no man that hath left house, or brethren, or sisters, or father, or mother, or wife, or children, or lands, for my sake, and the gospel's, but he shall receive an hundred fold now in this time houses, and brethren, and sisters, and fathers, and mothers, and children, and lands, with persecutions, in this life, and in the world to come eternal life".[1] "Eye hath not seen nor ear heard, neither hath it entered into the heart of man, the things which God hath prepared for them that love him."[2]

Jesus won Peter and Andrew, the fishermen, by promising to make them fishers of men.

Do you remember the story of his dealings with the woman at the well, in John 4?[3]

She is a Samaritan. She has come to the well for water. He reads at a glance that she is a prostitute.

First see what he does not do. He does not challenge her right away about her wrong living. He does not enter into or raise the theological differences between Jew and Samaritan.

First, he talks to her. This surprises her because

---

[1] Mark 10:29–30
[2] I Corinthians 2:9
[3] John 4:6–30

Jews did not talk to Samaritans, nor "good men" to prostitutes. He goes further. He asks her to give him a drink of water.

Jesus uses this simple point of contact. They talk about water. That is their common ground. Suddenly, by a natural transition, he is talking of a new kind of water, living water which he can give her. Those who drink it will never thirst again. Now she is fascinated. "Sir," says she, "give me this water, so that I need not thirst or come all this road to draw water."

Only now does Jesus move in with his challenge to her way of life. The rest of that matchless interview must be examined later in this book. Here be it simply noted that if Jesus, whose whole bearing spoke of power and love, needed carefully to think out his approach to this woman's soul, how much more must we?

To find a point of contact is often the first step in seeking friendship and trust. William Wilberforce, who through deliberate life-changing, gathered around him a team, more able, according to one historian, than any Prime Minister of the day could muster, went deliberately about it. Before seeing someone or going to a social occasion, he spent time thinking out "launchers", remarks which would lead the conversation to deeper levels. Yet he performed it so delicately that a contemporary said that at dinners "every face lit up with pleasure at his entry". It was this team that enabled him, in his life time, to abolish the slave trade and slavery and in many ways to "alter the morals of England".

The best way to give people a picture of the new life is often to bring them among those who are already living that life, in its full freedom and power. Then they can see from many angles, from men and women and children of every area, class and background, that the same great truths work out however different the circumstances.

But there will be many occasions when no such team is immediately available. Then the best way of getting across a picture of the new life, its happiness and its effect on large issues is by telling true stories. Stories of living people are the most useful, and probably the most neglected, of all the weapons. They can show the romance of the new life. They can picture the new spirit which can be brought into a community or even a nation, by the change in one or many people. They can give the dispirited person hope. The story of someone who has been in the same kind of difficulties as he or she but has come triumphantly through them, often makes that person say to himself, "Why, he is just like me. If he can find his way through by giving his life to God, perhaps I can too." Anyone who goes out trying to help people or situations without a number of stories is like a golfer who goes into a match with only one club.

So one is well advised to stock one's mind with stories. And more than that. You should work on them – writing them out, perhaps, in your own words – so that they become ready and suited to

Listening

your hand. Many people think that story-telling is a gift. No doubt it is – to be a Kipling or a Dickens. But even then it is ninety per cent hard work. Anyone, if he cares enough, can live into a story and bring it living before people's eyes. The first story to prepare is your own. If you once take the time and trouble to line it out in pictures, so that it is clear and even exciting, you will have a weapon of high calibre ready to hand. St. Paul must have felt this. The story of his change is told three times in the Acts alone.[1] But your own story may or may not be the first one to tell. It may be too intimate or too limited to begin with.

The greater experience of a team can be brought to a person's fireside through books. First there is the Bible team, Christ and the apostles, the people of Acts and of Israel, and often it is wise to introduce your friend to some modern translation so that the story may strike him fresh and new. Then there are the great documents of the past, the proved life-changing media down the ages, books like St. Augustine's "Confessions". But frequently, they will be too advanced for the seeker at this stage. Often it is better to start the seeker off with the experience, modernly presented, of modern people, whom he will immediately recognise as like himself. I had read the New Testament and knew most of the Old Testament stories, but I was not stirred to think the same thing could happen to me until I read "For Sinners

[1] Acts chapters 9, 22 and 26

Only",[1] a book talking about change in ordinary people in the world of that time.

* * * * * *

Establishing trust is only a stage in the winning of someone for God. It is the first mile, not journey's end; though often, when that mile is covered, the rest of the road is swiftly and readily trod.

There is no rule which will tell you when trust is established; just as there is no hard and fast division between this stage and those that follow. Some seed catalogues tell the gardener just how long each variety of plant will take to appear above the ground, to reach maturity, to be fit for gathering. Men and women defy such categories. But the Holy Spirit will surely tell the person who listens. The Spirit will call the pace at every step. Whether trust takes five minutes, five months or five years to establish, you must go at God's pace. The ambition that bids you press, the fear that cries "Hold back" must each be discarded.

An object lesson in such timing is to be found in the chapter "Bill Pickle" in "For Sinners Only". Frank Buchman[2] was working at an American university college. He was given a strategy for its transformation – three names which came morning by morning in his daily time of listening. The first was Bill Pickle,

---

[1] *For Sinners Only*, by A.J. Russell (Hodder & Stoughton, 1932).
[2] The initiator of the Oxford Group and Moral Re-Armament.

Listening

the local bootlegger, who during Prohibition supplied the students with liquor; the second a charming leader of the student body who called himself a Confucianist; the third the Dean, an agnostic. Buchman set himself to win their confidence.

It took many months of companionship and caring to break through the Confucianist's reserve. Buchman did not mention religion to him. Instead he walked with him, rode with him, holidayed with him; simply gave him affection and lived straight himself. Then one night, after a long day's riding, the Confucianist suddenly said, "Frank, will you tell me what Christ means to you?" That was the signal. That was the beginning of a new life and a companionship that lasted 50 years.

With Bill it was quite different. He had announced his intention of putting a knife in Buchman's back. But when Buchman, finding him drunk, and fighting, took him by the elbows and whispered in his ear, "Bill, we've been praying for you" – he fell still at once. He invited Buchman to his home, and very soon his confidence was firmly won, beginning with their joint interest in horses.

The strategy for the Dean was different again. Buchman never approached him. He simply went on bringing change to people all around him. Finally the Dean approached Frank, and asked him for the power which he saw demonstrated and did not understand. All three men were changed. The atmosphere of the college was transformed. Read the full story in "Remaking the World".[1] It will teach you much – and be another story you would find useful.

[1] pp 330–345. *Remaking the World* by Frank Buchman (Blandford, 1947).

Chapter Four
HONESTY BEGETS HONESTY

Roger Hicks is a cavalier of a man. He was at college some years before me.

Like Richard Lovelace, our college poet and predecessor, he would have fought for King Charles and Merrie England. I should have been for Cromwell and the Commons of Parliament.

Too late for this chance of expressing our rival temperaments, Roger and I sought and found other outlets. When I first heard of him, it was as the former leader of the high-living, fast-moving set in college. Secretly envying his freedom from convention, I affected the cloak of scorn.

After college Roger taught in a Christian college in India, immediately succeeding Malcolm Muggeridge. While on leave in England, he found a deeper experience. He became, and is today, a spiritual personality of grace, resolution and rare resourcefulness. Hundreds, in many lands, owe their faith and future to talks with him.[1]

One Christmas Roger led a foray to the slums of East London. On the first night he got talking to a gang of toughs on a pub corner. Casually he told

[1] Roger died in Australia, still on the job, in 1973.

them how he had stolen some money from one of his family.

The toughs, indifferent till then, sprang to life.

"What, Governor," said one of them, "you fiddled something?"

"Sure," said Roger.

"Well, as one crook to another, I sympathise," came the swift retort.

Roger had their confidence from that moment. And more. During the next weeks these fellows would not leave him alone. You would meet him walking with one of them any time of the day or night. They told him things they had not told their nearest friends.

This incident pictures for me the step in someone changing which follows the winning of his trust. It is the time when someone in need reveals the true nature of his malady. It is the period when symptoms are analysed, when defences are abandoned and two people seek together the root cause of the trouble. It is the crown and climax of trust, the threshold of decision.

Why do so few Christians take their friends to this place of healing honesty? Ninety times out of a hundred, I believe, it is because we will not do what Roger did – meet people "as one crook to another". We are not ready to use our own temptations and failures – past and present – to help the other person.

Consider this simple story.

When I was at school I had quite definite problems. I did not talk of them. I was ashamed of them. I made secret resolutions always succeeded by secret failures. Being as happy as, and more "successful" than, many of my fellows did not stop me worrying. I bottled up my afflictions and gradually came to think them unique.

I did once rouse the courage to tell someone these troubles. He was my house master. He had sat me down on the other side of his study fire for a pre-confirmation chat. I had great expectation of the ceremony. I yearned for a clean start. Somehow I blurted out the plain, common facts. I was so embarrassed that I felt a bit faint and had to bolt for a drink of water before I could proceed.

My house master was kind. He showed me to his private bathroom. I rejoined him with high hopes.

As I resumed my side of the fire, I was met with a flood of advice. It was kindly, for my house master was a good man and there was affection between us. But it was delivered from a height. And it was advice. There was no hint that he had ever been personally troubled by problems. There was no message of possible victory or personal experience in it. As I returned to my study, I felt empty and disillusioned. I decided being honest led you nowhere. I went on bottling things up for another four years – until I met Kit Prescott.

Kit took a different line. He diagnosed my trouble and frankly told me he had had the same problems. He had been beaten in the same struggle, but now, through the power he had found, he was free where he had been imprisoned.

Here was hope, and understanding. It seemed natural to tell him the truth. There was no need to defend myself to one who was careless of his own defences.

His secret? He had first been honest with me. He knew he could not expect me to start that painful, healthful process. So he started himself. He made my part easy.

Kit had learnt that you cannot live on a pedestal and help people in need at the same time. That is the great mistake of those who set out to "improve" their fellows. People don't like being "improved" or "reformed". Their hearts do not warm to those who seem to be shouting at them from on high, "Look how clean I am. Struggle up here beside me."

But we all welcome companions on the road. People respect those who are fighting their own battle of temptation far more than those who pretend they have no temptations at all, or at least none of a murky nature. Their reaction to such is that probably he is a liar, or if not that he is so unreal a being that he has nothing to give them. If, as is often the case, someone already feels his particular sin is peculiarly loathsome and even unique, his sense of hopelessness is only confirmed by being lectured.

The tragedy is that pedestal-squatters seldom see how pathetic they look up there, clinging to their little shreds of righteousness. I think of one man who had a real experience of Christ when he was seventeen. He is now thirty or forty years older, and that experience has been the basis of an upright and successful life. But when he talks of religion, everyone yawns. They know he had an experience all those years ago. They can only assume that he has been perfect ever since. They are incredulous, and bored. But they do not tell him. He is respected, but not loved. And lives are not changed around him.

Christ, mark you, did not feel himself fit for pedestal living. He used his temptations to help others. Else, how would we have heard of the forty days in the wilderness?

St. Peter must have shared with his friends the story of his denial. How else would we read of it? And the early Church must have felt it to be a helpful piece of witness or we should not find it related at such length in the Gospels.

The fact is that past sins, once faced and redeemed by God, are a priceless asset in helping others. They are our point of union with the person in need. It is folly not to make them work for God. St. Augustine knew this, and gives it as the main reason that he wrote the *Confessions*, considered by many the greatest Christian work outside the Bible. "People are curious," he says, "to pry into another's life, but reluctant to correct their own." But, he goes on, "The confession of my past sins, when people read or hear it, arouses the heart, no longer to slumber in despair and say, 'I can't', but to awaken to a love of your mercy and grace – your grace which makes the weak aware of his weakness and makes him strong."[1]

[1]*Confessions* Book 10, ch.III, 3 and 4

He had himself first been fired by the stories of others – a scholar, a civil servant, the monks in Egypt – who had discovered their faith and calling. St. Augustine did not spare himself in these confessions. He tells us the two events which hurt him most keenly and gave him the deepest sense of shame. Often it is the things of which we are most ashamed which help other people most.

Again, it is frequently the most recent victory over some sin or even the present struggle against one which is appropriate. It gives the other person the chance to help you, and life-changing is always best when it is a two-way affair.

Modern people want evidence. Preaching is apt to bore them. Advice makes them restive. Argument renders them bellicose. But evidence has to be considered in this age of experiments. And what evidence is as tangible as one's own experience of sin recognized, forgiven and left behind? The seeker can analyse that. He can test it. He can decide whether the person before him speaks truth or falsehood. But it must be evidence. Vague assurances that "Christianity is a great adventure" or "everything is wonderful now" do not impress. I heard many such assurances from pulpits at boarding school. Yet it never occurred to me that these men had any answer to my problems – which was then my only interest in religion.

Why do Christians so seldom give this specific evidence from their own lives?

In myself I find three reasons.

Honesty Begets Honesty 43

One: often I am afraid or just shy.

Two: if I am still playing with temptation myself, I naturally feel diffident of witnessing about a problem still unsolved.

Three: I love the warm, superior feeling which accompanies speaking down to people from a commanding height of my pedestal.

It is costly to step down, and be honest. No more comfortable glow. Also, if you know that at any moment you may have to use past or recent sins in helping others, it means you cannot tolerate the little compromises, the fluffy edges, that are so insidious because so small and attractive.

Many times pedestal-squatters have said to me, "My sins are between me and God." They are right. That is exactly where they are. They are also between them and their fellow men.

Be sure of this. If you descend from your pedestal, the rewards will be great. People will often say to you, "I don't know why I am telling you these things when I hardly know you . . ." Lives will be changed.

And, besides, you will have found the best antidote to the ever-present danger of becoming stuck-up. You will be kept in remembrance of and in clash with your own sins. You will begin to feel and pray in your heart with Paul "lest by any means, when I have preached to others, I myself should be a castaway."[1]

One word more. When you have made this

[1] I Corinthians 9:27

decision, be ready to share, but don't spill everything on everyone you meet. Nothing could be more boring. Be ready to share anything with anyone, when guided to do so. If you are ready, you will be told the when and the where and the how much.

Another fundamental lesson is not to be led into unnecessary arguments. People love arguing. Nothing would please them more than to contest whether stealing is permissible or not, or more generally whether the Devil exists or the Virgin Birth is credible.

Paul is outspoken on this subject in his letter to Timothy: "Remind men of this: adjure them before the Lord not to bandy arguments – no good comes out of that; it only means the undoing of your audience."[1]

The fact is that argument on points not relevant to them at the moment is a fine escape device. If someone wants to evade the search and sear of absolute moral principles, he often argues.

Read again the story of Christ and the woman at the well.[2]

Christ won her imagination by promising her living water. Then he moves on to put the moral test which alone has the salt and strength in it to cure her warped life. He tells her – a woman who has had five husbands and is living now with a man who is not her husband – to fetch her husband.

[1] 2 Timothy 2:14 (Moffat)
[2] John 4

Honesty Begets Honesty

What does she do?

She attempts denial but soon sees that is fruitless.

Her next line of defence is more adroit. She tries to draw Christ off by throwing a red herring across the scent.

She produces her theological difficulties. (It is amazing what unlikely people become theological when hard-pressed!) She is much concerned, she says, whether one should worship in Jerusalem or elsewhere. Now what does he think? He is evidently a prophet and must know about such things.

In fact, she raises one of the burning issues of the day, she hints that they as Jew and Samaritan are divided by race and intellectual convictions so that his message does not apply to her and she adds a dash of flattery to make good measure. Now ask yourself this – a kind of litmus-paper test for red herrings – would her problem be settled if she found an entirely satisfactory answer to her question? Would this woman have been any less promiscuous if she had been convinced that one should worship in Jerusalem?

Christ, of course, saw right through her antics. He brings the challenge, gently but firmly, back to her. "God is Spirit. He must be worshipped in Spirit and in reality."

The result? A whole village is shaken.

Red herrings will become familiar fish to every fisher of men. It is terribly tempting to get after them, especially when you feel you have a conclusive answer ready. But it is fatal to do so. You cannot reveal the unsearchable riches of Christ and your own cleverness at the same time.

Just let them pass. The other person knows he is trying to play you off. If he knows you know, all the charm goes out of the game. Back the conversation will come to the real issue, the place where the moral challenge confronts him.

Chapter Five
CONFESSION – WHY? HOW?

What is the point of confession? Why is it necessary?

Just as well ask why a patient should reveal to a doctor the exact location of his pain. Certainly no real Christian would wish to hear such confessions for their own sake. Henry Drummond once said to a friend: "Such tales of woe I've heard in this room that I have felt I must go and change my very clothes after the contact." Like the doctor, who enquires into the most loathsome symptom so as to make a sound cure, so he had tenderly to insist that the facts were in the open.

Experience shows that people who give their lives to God secretly seldom grow to full stature. Often this surrender is incomplete and is followed by disillusion – and danger of the seven devils moving in where one was before.[1] A person who allows people to shirk the full facing of their sins is likely soon to have spiritual deaths on his hands.

Those who insist that their sins are a secret between them and God seldom get beyond symptoms. The human power of self-deception is so infinite that the sad skeleton of lust (which a person

[1] Matthew 12:43–45

would spot instantly for what it is in others) seems to be a figure of alluring beauty, and even their fears can seem homely and familiar. We all need loving and disinterested friends who will help us see them as they really are, the blights of our lives.

Christ must have enjoined such openness upon his disciples, for they made it so central in their message. "If we say that we have fellowship with him and walk in darkness we lie and do not have the truth. But if we walk in the light we have fellowship one with another, and the blood of Jesus Christ his son cleanses us from all sin", St. John wrote in his first epistle.[1] And St. James concluded his epistle thus: "Confess your faults to one another, and pray for one another, that you may be healed."[2]

God alone can change someone. God alone can forgive him. Conviction of sin will best come as God speaks direct to the person himself. But someone who helps us to keep open to conviction and discard the automatic censoring machine which most of us have installed within to dilute any unpleasant truths about ourselves is very useful.

As Howard Walter, whose *Soul Surgery*[3] is a classic on the subject, wrote: "Not only is this entire self-disclosure needed in order that the spiritual surgeon may possess all the data for an accurate diagnosis. It is required by an imperious inner law that will not

---

[1] John 1:6 and 7
[2] James 5:16
[3] *Soul Surgery* (1919, Oxford)

leave to the sinner a vestige of the old prideful pose behind which he has shielded iniquity. The secret thing must be exposed before it can be dealt with effectually, permitting the sinner to go forward on a new basis of utter honesty, looking the whole world in the face."

Withal, do not underestimate the sheer relief that the honest telling brings to a person. And don't be afraid to ask questions which help him to get rid of the things he feels most ashamed of. In "For Sinners Only", Russell tells of a student who came to talk with Buchman about entering the Christian ministry.

"The student", says Russell, "had just attended a conference on the ministry at which brilliant addresses had interested but not convinced him . . . Frank answered his questions to the best of his ability, but still the man seemed unsatisfied. They had finished dinner with very little accomplished, and Frank then invited him to his room for further conversation. In time the student opened a little more and said, 'I'll tell you why I couldn't enter the ministry. I want my own way too much.'

" 'Isn't there anything else?' Frank asked, and the student said 'No'.

"Then Frank was told what he should say as suspicion became conviction; and leaning forward, he said quite naturally, 'Isn't your trouble . . .?'

"The barrier of pride crumbled away . . . and a new beginning was made on a sure foundation which transformed the young man . . . As they were walking together to the Underground, the student said (and it is worth remembering):

" 'Frank, I'd have cursed you tonight if you had not got at my real need.' "[1]

Two other rules for those who have to hear confessions are important.

1. *Never betray a confidence*. Obvious, you may say, but do not hurry over it on that account. It is quite fundamental. And often very difficult. Never to betray by word, or by deed the confidences reposed in you.

2. *Never betray an appearance of shocked surprise*. Shocked surprise closes a person's lips more quickly than anything. Canon B.H. Streeter, the late Provost of the Queen's College, Oxford, was insistent upon this point. He used to drive it home with a story against his own church. A murderer who was fleeing down a road in Oxford came to a Protestant church, rushed in and gasped out to the curate there: "Oh, sir, I have committed a murder." "Oh dear, oh dear," exclaimed the curate, running for the door, "I must

---

[1] In the sixties, a woman academic on a year's sabbatical from America kept coming to my wife, Margot, and complaining of the faults of her husband, also an academic. For many times Margot just listened. Then one day the thought came to ask the woman if she had ever given her life to God. Margot felt most embarrassed. The woman had been a Christian for forty years. Surely she must have given her life – she was loyal and so generous. However, in the end Margot put the question to her. "Given my life to God?" the woman replied. "Should I have done? I will with all my heart" – and she did so at once. From that time on her attitude to her husband and to life entirely changed.

fetch the vicar." The murderer followed him and ran on until he came to a Roman Catholic church. Here he found a priest and again gasped out his news. "How many times, my son?" said the priest.

But how to achieve unshockability?

Think of the case of the woman taken in adultery. The Pharisees were shocked. They were so shocked that they wanted to stone her. But when Jesus said: "He that is without sin amongst you, let him cast a stone at her", they all slunk away.[1] There is nothing like a just appreciation of your own character to make you unshockable.

[1] John 8:3–11

Chapter Six

WILLING TO WARN

Three wise words sum up the art of fishing for people. They all begin with W. They are: *Woo, Win, Warn*.

So far we have told of the wooing. And its importance is great. But it is still a part, not the whole. It is a means, not an end. To be content simply to woo is to imitate the fisherman who was an expert on bait but never caught a fish. When his more practical wife asked after his day's sport he would answer, "No, I didn't actually catch any. But I'm pretty certain I intrigued some and interested a great many."

Paul was a great wooer. His epistles were love letters. They are full of tenderness. They have warmed more hearts than the poems of Herrick. But they are also firm, sometimes even stern. For Paul was not one who loved with his eye cocked for the warm response. He loved too well to spare himself or others. He cared enough to cure.

His first letter to the Corinthians, with its wonderful thirteenth chapter about love, is the letter of a wooer. But it is also the letter of a warner. He cuts at the disease, clean and deep. His aim is to move his spiritual children on to that place of pain and promise which is called conviction of sin.

When he writes again a year later he explains the thought and feeling behind his original letter. "If I did pain you by that letter", he writes, "I do not regret it. I did regret it when I discovered that my letter had pained you even for the time being but I am glad now – not glad that you were pained, but glad that your pain induced you to repent. For you were pained as God meant you to be pained, and so got no harm from what I did; the pain God is allowed to guide ends in a saving repentance never to be regretted."[1]

Paul did not enjoy hurting his friends. He knew the sting of it too well himself. For you cannot be used to bring conviction of sin to others unless you often and sharply experience it yourself. Paul felt the barb in his own flesh even as he launched it. "My little children of whom I travail in birth again until Christ be formed in you . . ."[2]

But Paul knew too that conviction is the only way to a fuller and freer life. So he set himself to bring it. His concern was that God should dominate and direct the whole process – that his own words to the Corinthians should be so God-guided that, in their turn, his readers would allow God to guide them to a saving repentance never to be regretted.

Everyone gets conviction of sin sometimes. The test is what we do with it. If we accept and carry it through to repentance, we shall receive life and know

[1] 2 Corinthians 7:8–10 (Moffat)
[2] Galatians 4:19

Willing to Warn

progress. If we slough it off or stifle it in remorse, spiritual decay will follow as surely as night succeeds twilight.

What is the difference between remorse and repentance? A boy's definition is the best I know. "Remorse is when you are sorry about something, but go and do it again. Repentance is when you are sorry enough to quit." Remorse is often accompanied by self-pity. Also by a frantic desire to recoup, to pull oneself up by one's own bootlaces and no interference from God, please. Repentance on the other hand brings the sharp insight that the particular sin is only a symptom of the disease that is me without Christ – and that my need is a cure, a change of character, deeper than any self-effort can produce.

Nathan had brought King David to that point when he wrote the fifty-first Psalm. David makes no grudging admission. He does not cavil. "I acknowledge my transgressions and my sin is ever before me . . ." He knows that redemption is beyond his power. "Wash me thoroughly from mine iniquity and cleanse me from my sin. Purge me with hyssop and I shall be clean . . . Create in me a clean heart and renew a right spirit in me."

It is a shattering realisation, and people commonly bring to bear every defensive weapon to save themselves from it. You can see the defensive screen around them like the anti-aircraft barrage over a bombed city.

The barrage may take many forms. One form is angry denial. Another is strategic acquiescence. A third may be called the "mathematical escape". All are symptoms of the mighty arguments going on in one's heart.

In 1937 I went to New York with a great trust from my co-workers. It was to help give a shaped message, in magazine form, to the American people. I was not keen on going. I had been in love with Margot for some years, and she, I sensed, with me. But I had had the clear thought, which I knew God had given me, not to mention it to her. One afternoon a few weeks earlier, we had, however talked to each other of our feelings, which was, for me, a deliberate disobedience of that direction. I immediately became too preoccupied with the desire to marry Margot immediately.

So when a cable came inviting me to America, I was extremely reluctant to go. My friends in England warmly agreed that I should go, and when I listened to God it was clear to me that I should do so. Deep down, however, I felt the trip was not so much a commission to do a job as a strategem of God or man to part me from Margot.

The magazine had been designed in Britain by an international group. I was to take a packet of vital photographs and help with the editing. I was so preoccupied with my distaste at going that, on leaving Waterloo for Southampton, I forgot to get the packet from the man who was seeing me off. I only missed it after the boat had sailed, and was more than relieved when the packet was brought to me when we were well out in Southampton water.

Willing to Warn

Someone had raced down by car from London and just caught the pilot's launch.

My friends in New York received me warmly, and I, for my part, plunged into the work to drown my sorrows. I did not tell them what I was up against, and acquiesced in their adaptations to the original conception which I had been sent to put through. We worked 18 hours a day and produced something which was a commercial success, but at certain points lacked the challenge of the original. We were rather pleased with ourselves.

Meanwhile, my failure to face my real problem caught up with me. Power to help people dwindled to a trickle. I became restless, afraid of what people thought of me.

Meanwhile, three thousand miles away, one of the friends who had commissioned me had had a clear thought about my condition. He sent me a cable which seemed frank, even merciless. I see now that it was of armour-piercing calibre because he knew my heart was armour-plated.

That was the end of acquiescence. I tried the second popular escape – surly anger. The cable arrived the day before Christmas, two days before my birthday. That was another grievance.

Now my cry was 'injustice'. I mumbled bitterly to myself about people not understanding. I tried with the mathematical escape too – that is trying to decide exactly what percentage of the failure was due to me, and what percentage of what had been said to me I could reject as wrong. If I saw I was ninety per cent wrong, why then I was ten per cent right, and they were ten per cent wrong, and I concentrated on that.

I write these reactions at length, because they are so common in those battling with conviction of sin. We must learn to recognize them and be ready to deal with them. Our job is to assist the friend on to the real conviction and repentance which brings freedom.

Now, how did real conviction come to my heart?

I went away alone one day, my mind milling round and round with grudging calculations, and decided simply that I would see the matter through, then, once and for all. I knelt down and asked God to convict me at the heart.

Until then my problems had seemed numerous, formidable, and unpassable as the Himalayas. Then it dawned on me. I had only one problem. My contact with God had snapped. I determined to re-establish it, fresh and clear, whatever the cost.

Very quickly my eyes were opened. I saw that at every failure I had said: "Yes, yes, bad of course. But it is an exception. I still have my good points. The admirable, the essential Garth marches on."

At every fresh assault on the walls of my empire I retreated to a prepared position – the inner citadel of self-esteem. The citadel got smaller and smaller. But it was still there, warm and comforting.

Now I saw that the citadel itself was rotten. These failures were not exceptions. They were a perfect expression of me. They were, and are, Garth without Christ. The thought came, "You are like a woman

Willing to Warn

who hugs her baby so close that it suffocates. That is what you have done with your love for Margot. You destroy what you treasure most, and others suffer from your neglect."

Repentance was begun at last. Conviction remained, and grew, from day to day as I saw the harm I had done to others by my selfishness. I was brought daily into violent collision with the way I had starved my best friends of affection and help. But from now on conviction was progress. I was glad to see each new sin, because Christ was real to me again and I knew they could be cured.

I had learnt the relationship with Christ which has to be constant if victory is to be constant.

> "Nothing in my hand I bring,
> Simply to Thy Cross I cling;
> Naked, come to Thee for dress;
> Helpless, look to Thee for grace;
> Foul, I to the fountain fly;
> Wash me, Saviour, or I die."

"Foul, I to the fountain fly." How hardly I came to that simple truth. It was the key to new life. It is a place to which I have had to come again and again.

Often at this point it looks as if one has come up against a blank wall, and that admission of one's failure is the end of everything. But when one has accepted it and made any decisions which come from it, a door opens through the wall – and a greater vista than ever before will lie before you.

Chapter Seven
FACING THE TRUTH

You will readily understand that this stage of conviction is apt to be the most critical moment of anyone's change. If we accept the truth and ask God to deal with it, new life opens up. If we do not, we are all too apt to turn on anyone who is trying to help us – or even on God – and to do all we can to prove to ourselves and others that we are quite all right as we are. Sometimes people even get to the point of inventing strange stories or even scandals about those who have questioned their attitudes.

We need to understand this. Do not be surprised or scared if you hear your friend is spreading rumours about you, or if he suddenly hives off and avoids your company. And be sure your reaction is dictated by God, not by hurt feelings.

This soreness which is a symptom of this stage lays added responsibilities on you. But do not confuse the soreness of genuine conviction with annoyance caused by your clumsiness – for example, through the raising of false issues or trying to dominate. Your prime job is to help your friend give the Holy Spirit the chance to speak to *him*, not to try and make him follow your own ideas.

So at this stage – and indeed at almost any stage

– it is good to suggest that you should listen to God together. Very often those who are shy of prayer will readily agree to make this practical experiment.

Or it may be that your friend will go away to listen in the privacy of his own room.

In either case it is often helpful to suggest that, in this first quiet time, he takes four pieces of paper, puts one of the absolute standards – absolute honesty, purity, unselfishness and love – on the top of each, and asks God to reveal to him any places he falls short of them. What will need to come into his life and what will need to go out of it, if he is to be Christ's man?

Often such a time of quiet will take place unsuggested as you talk together. One of those living silences will fall in which a person searches his heart, and hears the voice of God. Beware of the temptation to chatter away the awkwardness. If you keep quiet and pray – even if it is for many minutes – it may be the turning point.

Don't be discouraged or fooled if your friend says God has said nothing in his time of listening. Sometimes people are reluctant to recognize the thoughts of God – or conscience – when they come. A woman once told a friend of mine, Francis Goulding, that she could get no guidance. "Didn't you get any thoughts?" asked Francis.

"No", said she.

"None at all?"

"Well there were a few letters to write to people I

had gossiped about. But you would not call that guidance."

"How many?"

"Oh, about thirty-five."

"How long would that take?"

"About two weeks."

"Well", said Francis, "it seems to me that you have enough guidance to last you two weeks."

Kit Prescott, on the other hand, recognised his first thoughts in quiet as coming from God; though he too at first denied their existence just because they had been so straight and clear.

He had been brought to an Oxford Group meeting by his sister, Dorothy, and had taken the precaution to get well-oiled beforehand. The meeting was being led by the Rev. Julian Thornton-Duesbery, later Master of St. Peter's Hall, Oxford. Afterwards Kit's sister introduced them to each other – and left them together.

Kit, according to Julian, began talking, almost shouting at him. He continued for three quarters of an hour, denouncing religion in general and the Oxford Group in particular.

Julian just smiled. Then he said, "Well, suppose we listen to God together."

"All right," said Kit, rather taken aback, "But I shan't get anything."

They listened for five minutes. Then Julian asked Kit what had come to him.

"Nothing," was the reply, "Nothing at all."

"Well," said Julian, "Two things come to me. First

the words 'You can't serve God and Mammon', and second that you should give your life to God tonight."

Kit was astonished. He had had those very same thoughts. He went away, and that night, in his own room gave his life to God.

God will define the issue. When that has happened, you must hold hard. Do not shrink. Do not lower the hurdles. If you do you may get a smile of momentary relief, but you will lose your friend.

I think of my dealings with a certain author. He came to me for help. He told me his main problem – and gave me clearly to understand that he wanted to live a spiritual life in every area except that one.

I was flattered by his liking for me. I enjoyed his company. So I told him my view of his problem, but then I let it lie. I said to myself: "I have made my position clear. Now he will just go along. One day he will be willing. The main thing is for me to retain his friendship."

For a year we continued. Then through someone else he came up against the full challenge of faith. He would not face it. He disappeared.

Two years passed, and a time of persecution came for the Oxford Group. The author vented his disappointment in a newspaper article. Characteristically he did not attack me, who had failed him. He attacked a man, whom he had only twice met for a few minutes, and who he must have sensed would not let softness blur the integrity of his commitment.

No. Your vocation is not to dilute the conviction,

but to bring it home to your friend so that he may be fundamentally cured.

One way is to help him see the pain and damage his sin has wrought in other people's lives. As Saul Kane says in Masefield's "The Everlasting Mercy" –

"That old mother made me see
 The harm I'd done by being me."

Often conviction comes when a man or woman considers what they have done to their family.

Arthur is a respected member of a great profession. He holds one of the highest positions of its kind in the land, and the company with which he is associated has a world-wide reputation for stability and respectability.

When he came to a gathering some years ago he seemed to have every virtue except a sense of sin. He was a good fellow, everyone liked him, and he looked blandly at such standards as absolute honesty and purity and said that there was nothing much to worry him there. Perhaps there was a little money owing, etc., but he did not need God to show him that. He had only come to this gathering, said he, because he was worried about his son, a lad of fourteen who had just run away from school.

During that week-end God spoke to Arthur. He told him that his love for comfort had bred his boy's indiscipline, his temper the boy's rebellion, his softness the boy's softness.

Arthur gave his life to God. Every important step in his spiritual development through the years has come from some further vision of where he can find fuller grace in order to give more fully to the family. Britain has cause to be grateful for him. Many men of affairs go to their work with clearer heads and cleaner hearts because of talks with him.

As I write this chapter another example is given me.

A business man recently came to see me and told me his sorry case. He was very busy. You see, in addition to his work he had all the housework to do. His wife had serious nervous trouble. Fear, he supposed. No, he could do nothing. He was a good Christian and would not wilfully harm anyone. That was his code. It worked very well.

Yet his face was ploughed with the deep, twisted furrows of fear.

After listening for an hour to a not unflattering account of his character by himself, it came to me to say, "I believe your wife would get much better if you found the answer to your fears. You are a fearful man, aren't you?"

"Nothing of the sort," said he.

"Think it over," I had to answer. "How many of her fears has your wife caught from you?"

He went away angry. But a few days later he returned looking ten years younger. He had fought against conviction, but whenever he sat opposite his wife, he had seen himself mirrored in her. A new life started for both of them. Both are growing strong.

People are often helped to a true picture of themselves by considering how much – or little – positive help they give to others. Not just material help – that is important, but can be a "buy off" for the spiritual help which we all feel instinctively we should be able to give.

George Marjoribanks, the seventh generation of the Scots manse, had his most rewarding experience when he saw that his contribution to his college could be summed up thus: "My friends cannot make me drunk. But I cannot make them sober." After giving his life wholly to God, George became one who helped people with rare sensitivity.

It was the same conviction that brought Dr. Foss Westcott, Metropolitan of India, Burma and Ceylon, to a new and more adventurous spiritual practice. That saintly and humble bishop came to Oxford for the celebrations of the Oxford Movement's anniversary and visited us at Lady Margaret Hall. Everyone loved him. Nobody kowtowed to him. He felt one of the family from the start.

After a time he spoke about a conviction which God had given him – that he had not basically helped individuals around him. On the boat to England he had not had one vital Christian talk ending in a decision in the other's life. When he travelled back to India, some months later, no less than fourteen of those he met on board ship – including planters whom he would never have approached – gave their lives to God with him.

Foss Westcott today is a firm believer in the principle that if you are not winning new people to faith you are sinning somewhere. "It is something I was never taught at my theological college, nor asked about by the Mission Board," he told me once. "It is a test every Christian should put to himself."

Another service which you may do to your friend is to help him to see the mechanism of sin and its effect on himself, his community, and the nation.

Few people see with what deadly power sin works. Fifty years ago there were standards in life. People did not always observe them. But they knew they had done wrong if they broke them. Today there are no universally accepted standards.[1] Many are frankly given over to doing whatever they wish, and any standard that exists is a relative one. Very commonly people say: "What does it matter what I do provided I don't hurt someone else?" And they, be it noted, judge whether the other person has been hurt.

The fact is that, whatever their political opinions, most people are pacifists in the war against sin. Yet we are in the battle whether we like it or not. If we do not clash with it, our view of sin soon becomes as unreal as is the soldier who does not believe there is any such thing as live ammunition.

Someone once summarised the effect of sin in four words. "Sin binds, blinds, deadens and multiplies."

Sin binds. Have you noticed that those who talk most of their right to freedom to live as they please often end up the most imprisoned of people? In "freeing" themselves from "convention" they tie themselves to their indulgence. The Devil so arranges it that every sin looks at the beginning like a new

[1] Still more true now, in 1990

Facing The Truth

and grand step to liberty. But soon it has control of you, instead of you controlling it. "Sow a thought, reap an act; sow an act, reap a habit; sow a habit, reap a character; sow a character, reap a destiny." That works negatively as well as positively, nationally as well as personally. As nine year old Elizabeth said, "God's guidance begins rather difficult but ends lovely. Satan's guidance begins nice but ends nasty, like eating too much for tea and finishing with a tummy-ache."

Sin blinds. Very soon a person who gives way to a sin becomes blind to his condition. That is the tragedy. He walks about proclaiming in every word and action his defeat. Others see it. He does not. "Love's blind, but the neighbours ain't."

But it is not only to himself that he is blind. Sin warps judgement. Take temper, for instance. Be you cabinet minister or cabinet maker you cannot keep losing your temper without your judgement suffering. Nor can you overdrink or sleep around and at the same time give the family or the nation what they need. Sin is the greatest reason for failure in many an enterprise.

Sin deadens. Many are so sunk that they no longer expect victory. They regard any attempt to live a life of complete faith as abnormal. But God made the world to run that way. We who have tried to run it on subnormal lines are the ones who have run it into disaster.

Take marriage. How many couples keep through life the bright hopes of the first days? Or how many accept as inevitable the dull, shabby, shoddy thing it has become, get divorced in the hope they'll have better luck next time?

The fact is that sin dulls and deadens the creative faculties. It cuts you off from the source of inspiration – the Holy Spirit. That was our condition between the wars. Statesmen and people are uncreative when they are deadened to God's guidance and the prevision that He gives.

Sin multiplies. It passes from person to person. It catches like an infection. And one sin leads to another. As I am, so is my nation. You cannot have smallpox and not endanger your nearest and dearest. Likewise with sin. The theory that you can sin and hurt no one else is convenient – but untrue. Also, when sin is normal to many in the media, they preach it to millions.

* * * * * *

Any of these things may help your friend. But I repeat that only the Holy Spirit can give to him the conviction that he needs. Only the Spirit can force a way into people's hearts and make them see themselves with new eyes. And it is more important that they should have one such God-given conviction and carry it through to change than that you should take people through any human examination or rigmarole. Here, as ever, the only safe course is to listen day by day and minute by minute to God's direction – and to be honest about, and let God deal with, our

Facing The Truth

own sins. Often people are more interested in our present temptations, and how we are dealing with them than with what happened to us long ago.

* * * * * *

It is helpful to remember that there is a happier sequence of events than that outlined above. The opposite of sin is not sinlessness or perfection, but forgiveness. Forgiveness, as I hope I have already shown, makes you free. It also gives you insight and makes you come alive. Again, it has an infectious quality about it. It is the basis of all the great awakenings in history. Once forgiveness is accepted, the Holy Spirit goes to work all round you. And it is only when we limit him by our fears or inconsistencies that people cease to change around us.

Chapter Eight
DECISION

The heart of the matter is a voluntary decision of the will. It can take place in many ways.

In New York, in 1936, I met a man in Reuters who was in a mess. He got out of it, which interested the chief International Affairs columnist of another great agency, whom I will call Fraser. Fraser asked an American friend of mine, Dubois Morris, and me to lunch.

Seeing we were young enough to be his sons, Fraser started by trying to shock us. He described the tough newspaper world of New York, stressing his drinking and womanising. "Why should I want to change?" he asked, "I've got all the women I want, all the money I want, all the drink I want."

"Yes," said Morris, "and you're empty."

Fraser went back to the office, and we began to pray about him. The next Saturday, when I was listening to God in the early morning, I had the thought, "Spend this afternoon with Fraser".

I rang him up. He said he was busy that afternoon. But though he said "No", he meant "Yes". I held on, and suddenly he said, "All right, be at the office at four." I was, and he took me across Madison Avenue to a hotel.

"I'll never forgive you for what you've done to me," Fraser said, as we went down.

"What's that?"

"You've made me feel damned uncomfortable."

"Perhaps it's about time."

"I'm not going to change," he said, aggressively.

"I never asked you to," I replied.

Over tea Fraser began to tell me about his life. The son of a Presbyterian Minister in Vermont, he had gone early into journalism. He had been a war correspondent on the Western Front in World War 1, and after that chief of his agency's London Bureau. He loved writing and hated administration, and so had gone back to New York to be a foreign affairs analyst. He was the first man to do a signed column on foreign affairs for his agency. It went to over a thousand papers across America and the world each day.

While in London, his first wife had died. He had fallen in love with an English actress, and they married. They now had two children.

Fraser was in love with his wife, Dorothy, but he was married to his column. All the years I have known him he has been going to get a few days ahead with it. He never has. It is hard to get ahead with a foreign affairs column.

He sometimes neglected Dorothy. He was often away for long periods and was pre-occupied when at home. Six months before I met him, he had come back from a trip to South America. They had had a quarrel. She said she was tired of being left alone so much. He fired back. She flashed back that he was not the only pebble on the beach. He was furious.

Dorothy took the children to her parents in England. Fraser, with the dour self-righteousness of his kind, felt she alone was guilty, and swore that if he ever discovered the man in the case, he would break him.

To forget Dorothy – and, in one way, to revenge himself upon her – he was chasing the girls and drinking heavily. Some people in the office said he was losing his grip. He denied this, but I could see he was worried.

Beside this man of the world, my experience of life as meagre. I knew nothing of the world in which he moved, nor had I ever slept with a woman. But I knew the pull of greed, resentment and lust as well as anyone, and had found that there was a power which enabled me to resist temptations which had beaten me before. I told Fraser this – and also that I believed God had a plan for each man, which meant fulfilment, not frustration.

"I'm not going to change," he announced belligerently as we parted.

"That's your funeral," I replied.

Three mornings later, at seven o'clock, Fraser rang up. "I've decided to square things up," he said.

I asked when we could meet. He said he'd see me in a week's time. "Until then you can do any long distance work you like (he meant prayer) but no short distance work. I want to see how it goes."

We met as arranged in a Turkish restaurant, Fraser,

Morris and I. He told us he had been drunk the night after I had seen him, and the next night too. On the third morning he had woken with the certainty that God was there. Three clear thoughts came forcefully to him: "Stop drinking. Stop smoking. Stop womanising."

"It's odd," he told us. "You never said any of these things were wrong. I just knew they were wrong for me. I decided to obey."

Since then he had been to the same parties, met the same women and carried an open packet of cigarettes in his pocket. He took it out and showed it to us. "I haven't wanted any of them," he said. Later that day he confirmed before us his decision to give his life to God.

Soon after this, we suggested to Fraser that he might need to think where he was to blame with Dorothy. He did not like that idea. "I'll never forgive her," he said.

"It may be you who needs the forgiveness," we replied.

Three weeks later Fraser phoned me and asked me to pray for him. "I'm in great trouble," he said. I went round to his rather sleazy hotel. He was in bed with lumbago – and in considerable mental stress. He would not tell me what was wrong. All he would say – and he repeated it over and over again – was, "It might have happened in a play."

Into my head, unbidden, rushed the thought that he had discovered the third person in the triangle – and that it was his close friend, a high official in his news agency whom I will call Crofts. At the same moment, Fraser said: "You know what it is, don't you, Garth? Go and deal with it."

No further word was spoken. I was in a dilemma. Should I go home and leave Fraser to get out of his own mess? Or should I play my hunch – and go and suggest to a man twice my age, a distinguished-looking and respected fellow, that he had been having an affair with his best friend's wife? I was frightened, but I decided I had to take the risk.

I went to the place where Crofts generally took lunch. We talked. It was true, and he was terrified. He knew Fraser intended to break the other man if he ever found him. Indeed, Fraser had often told him so. He knew Fraser was a dour, determined, unforgiving man, and believed Fraser could get him turned out of his job by complaining to the head of the agency. For Fraser was very close to the Managing Director. Also, Fraser was a big man and might be violent.

That evening I took Crofts to Fraser. They talked alone. To my astonishment, they were still friends at the end of it. Fraser came to see in those next days how he had treated Dorothy. He wrote to her in England, asking her forgiveness for the past, and whether she would come back to him.

In the middle of the Atlantic – there was no airmail then – a letter from her crossed his. "For the sake of the children," she wrote, "could we not have one more try?"

Dorothy came alone at first, then with the children. They rebuilt their home and it has lasted.[1]

The change in the Frasers caused comment in a society where homes often break and are seldom mended. The Secretary of State, Cordell Hull, asked Fraser about it. He had noticed that Fraser's words kept their nip, but lost their acid, a matter of importance in perhaps the most widely-read foreign affairs analyst of his day.

Something deep had happened to Crofts too. When I left America some months later, he telegraphed me on board ship: "Goodbye and may you have a happy and successful trip. The experiences you brought me will always be a landmark of my life and you have my heart's gratitude."

It was the story of Fraser and Crofts which I told to Peter Howard when, in 1940, we had tea together in a cafe in Fleet St. Howard, at the time, was a highly successful political columnist in the Sunday Express and writer for Beaverbrook's other London newspaper. He had been personally trained by Beaverbrook and was, on many occasions, his political voice. At this point, Beaverbrook had joined Churchill's cabinet and had sent down orders that Howard was not to write about politics while he was in the cabinet.

Howard was furious and was besieging the Managing Director to get the order cancelled, for he regarded the political column as his power base. The

---

[1] It lasted for the rest of their lives and they influenced many.

Decision

Managing Director's secretary, Mrs. Ducé, as the buffer between Howard and her boss, bore the brunt of Howard's displeasure. She told him in one of their tussles that he ought to come and see me because I "would help him".

To my surprise Howard did telephone me and asked that we meet. Most of my Fleet St friends advised me to refuse, saying Howard was the most dangerous journalist in London; and I was aware that, deprived of the politicians, he was more likely to be looking for other victims than any spiritual help. However, I decided to go. The thought which came to me was to tell him one story, and then leave. This annoyed him, and, as I rose to go, he insisted that we had not talked at all and must meet again. We fixed to have lunch the next Wednesday.

Naturally, I prayed hard what I should say at that lunch, for I knew that this time it could not be a matter of gulping and going. The only thought that came to me as I listened in the morning was, "Tell Howard he is as selfish as hell, because when men are dying in the war, all he seems to care about is his career." You can imagine that it was with some apprehension that I set out for that lunch.

We ate in a flat I had borrowed from a friend in the Temple, and, having nothing else to say, I began almost at once by telling him the thought that had come to me about him.

In the heat of the moment, Howard seemed to forget that he had sought me out to get an exposé of my work, and replied "What do you suggest that I do about it?"

"You ought to change," I said. "At a time of crisis like this, the country can't afford to have men in your position with such a small aim."

"What do you mean?" he replied, "A man can't change just like that."

"Of course he can," I said, "God can change you, whenever you like."

"But I don't believe in God," he answered, as though that settled the matter.

"That does not alter God's position in the least. He doesn't depend on whether you believe in him. He is either there or he isn't, and you can easily find out."

I added that you did not have to believe in electricity to find out if it was there. All you had to do was to turn on the light switch. He seemed interested and asked me how I had made my own first experiment eight years earlier.

While we talked I was praying rather desperately to be told what to do or say next. For I was aware that this talk bade fair to end up in half a column of ridicule in the Express, and I knew that humanly I could do nothing to prevent it. Howard was cleverer than I and had a great newspaper behind him.

The thought which began to come with compelling force was to ask Howard to pray with me. I thought this was crazy and resisted it. I pictured the way it could be used in the paper. But it kept coming and in the end I knew I had to risk it.

"There's a very simple way of discovering whether God exists or not", I told him.

"What's that?"

"If you ask God to come into your life and change it, he will either come or not. If he does, you'll know. If he doesn't you can always go on living the way you live now."

There was a long silence.

"Well," I gulped, "Would you like to ask him now?"

To my astonishment, Howard said he would and got down on his knees in that King's Bench Walk flat. I followed.

Just then, there came a heavy foot on the ancient oak staircase leading to our and other flats. Howard leapt to his feet. I stayed where I was. The foot-steps went up beyond our door. Howard got down on his knees again and began to pray. I don't remember his exact words. He asked God, if he was there, to tell him what to do – and he would do it.

Peter, as he soon became to me, later wrote that he went through this process because he thought it would win my confidence and open to him the inner workings of what some of us were doing. I was aware of this possible motive, but felt at peace because the contract he had made was not with me, but with God. And God is apt to take you at your word.

I saw him most days after that, and his thoughts when he listened in the early morning, besides telling him to change his ways in the office and not be bitter, involved several costly financial acts of restitution. When he paid back £150 in one of them, I felt sure he was serious, and even when, a little later, he refused to see me for a fortnight because God had asked him to be honest with his wife, I still felt sure that all was well. And, indeed, it was. The change, of course, created a sensation in Fleet St and ultimately he gave up his well-paid job rather than truckle down to immoral orders.[1] He came to work with some of us full time without pay.

Neither Fraser nor Crofts nor Howard knew the rationale of conversion when they started. They did not need to. They only needed to make the decision of the will which releases the eternal engine of conversion – the pent-up power of the Atonement, God's infinite love, forgiveness and grace in the remaking of lives. "Whoever has the will to do the will of God," said Jesus, "shall know whether my teaching is from him."[2]

To make that decision you do not even have to be sure that God exists. It is the most golden promise for the future, and the unique quality of His love, that He waits, always ready to prove His power in us when we take the decision which calls Him in.

---

[1] In the next twenty-five years he became a Christian statesman of rare sensitivity, vision and effectiveness. On 22 May 1969 – four years after his untimely death – *The Daily Telegraph* wrote of him, "There seems, indeed, to have been few more remarkable conversions since St Paul of Tarsus set out for Damascus." Needless to say, he taught me far more than I had ever taught him.
[2] John 7:17

Decision

This decision is an act of faith, not an act of certainty. Faith does not come from sitting still until you are sure you can act without risk. It means doing the thing which will make you ridiculous or lost, if God does not intervene. It is betting your life that there is a God of love and power.

In both the instances related in this chapter, the time of decision was brief, but, in fact, it varies widely from a day to twenty years to never – in this life at least. The greatest life-changers whom I have known – if I may return to Jesus' fishing metaphor – have had dozens, even hundreds, of lines out. They are always ready to accept anyone at his or her own time. Their priority meanwhile is to remain loyal friends whatever the outcome. In my wife's case, however, she was helped not to put off decision for weeks or months, which might have become never, by a friend reminding her that it was not her time she was wasting, but God's.

* * * * * *

B.H. Streeter, in *The God Who Speaks*, outlines a simple way of starting a new life, appropriate for anyone. "We all know at least one thing in our lives which is *not* right: and what is meant by wrong or sin, except thought or action which is contrary to God's will, that is, to God's plan for us? Until and unless he has straightened out that wrong, it is profitless to ask what may be the next item in God's plan for him. If, however, we are ready to conform to God's plan in this one respect in which we know it, then experience shows that 'the still small voice' of 'the Beyond that is within' will tell us the next thing that God wishes us to do."

Chapter Nine
PUTTING THINGS RIGHT

Would I bet my life on an uncertainty? This question was painfully clear to me, as I sat with Kit Prescott that afternoon in his little room near college. He spoke of God's absolute moral standards and told me that I must consider the cost and decide whether or not I was going to give my life to God.

I protested that God was just a vague, oblong blur to me. Kit had seen that red herring before. He smiled and said not a word.

What proof had he that God existed? I asked. He smiled again. "That is no proof," I cried angrily.

"You will get your proof *after* you have acted," replied Kit.

I remember thinking at the time of the short-sighted and probably mythical master famed in the legend of my school. The story went that he had one dark night determined to take a swim. He groped his way to the school swimming bath, mounted the high dive and committed himself to the air. At the inquest it was explained that the bath had been emptied that afternoon for cleaning.

There I was on the high dive. And I had this advantage over my late lamented schoolmaster. I could hear Kit and his friends down below, splashing in the water and shouting, "Come on in, the water's fine." But it was dark. I could not see at all. They *might* just be splashing their fingers in buckets to deceive me.

I took another look at Kit. I felt sure that he was honest, that he had something I wanted. It was on his faith that I jumped – strictly in an experiment based on my faith in him and his faith in God.

What action was involved for me? First of all I knelt down with Kit and told God simply that I gave my life to him – if he would make clear to me what he wished me to do, then I would do it.

There was nothing emotional about it. It was an act of the will. I was studying law at the time and it appealed to me as a cold, common sense contract.

I have said that I felt fear as I stood on that high dive. Was it just fear of the unknown?

No. Much was fear of the well-known.

For Kit had given me this thought: "If you will put right what you can put right, God will put right what you can't put right."

Restitution. That was the action I had to take. Wherever I could do anything to right the wrongs I had done I must do it. It has been said that you should do four things with sin – hate it, forsake it, confess it, restore for it. I had to restore for mine.

At this time my most treasured possession was the good opinion of two of my brothers. They were six and four years older than me respectively. I had grown up in love and awe of them. I had read their books, and appropriated their opinions as my own.

Putting Things Right

Neither professed belief in Christ. One of them was aggressively agnostic.

My first thought on listening had been about these two. It came back to me that I had stolen a pound from one and had been in the habit of reading the private correspondence of the other. God said I must apologise and restore as far as I was able.

There was no escaping it. God's searchlight beam kept playing upon them. This action was for me as definite a test as Christ's command to the blind man to bathe his eyes in the pool of Siloam or to the rich young ruler to sell all he had. My decision pivoted on them. As I knelt down and gave my life to God I knew that I was first of all deciding to send those letters to my brothers.

No one pretends making restitution is a pleasant business. Veterans of Dunkirk have told me that they would rather face a tank than a sticky apology. I remember myself how when I had dropped those letters into the college letter box I would have given anything to have them back again. No, restitution is not pleasant. But it is productive.

It produces a peaceful mind. Someone described it as letting the cat out of the bag before someone else does it for you, by which time there would have been kittens. What a relief it is to have nothing to hide, nothing in your life, past or present, that you mind anyone finding out. You feel like Christian in "Pilgrim's Progress" when he dumped his load.

Restitution demonstrates the reality of the desire to change, and God always honours it. When Zacchaeus, the ex-taxgatherer stated that he would restore four-fold to anyone he had swindled and would give half his goods to the poor, Jesus exclaimed: "This day is salvation come to this house."[1]

It also creates new relationships. For if God tells you to restore to someone, He has often prepared the other person and uses it in that person's life.

I think of one of those in college to whom I had to apologise.

He was from a North Country grammar school. He had a strong accent and a personal conceit which made him the butt of the "smart" public school set. I affected to resent this, and used to defend him sometimes. I told his aggressors that they were snobs. But that did not prevent me from playing a trick on him which gained the laughter and congratulation of this set, while leaving him ignorant who had harmed him. I was intensely ashamed of my hypocrisy and meanness. I hated the thought of admitting that I was the author of the "joke". I argued that it was ancient history, that I would never do it again. But my orders came sharp and clear. I had to obey.

When I did, he was furious. "Go to hell," he said. That experiment did not seem to have been a great success.

Some time later, however, I had the persistent thought that I should ask him to coffee with me

[1] Luke 19:9

Putting Things Right

that evening. He angrily refused."You have a perfect right to feel as you do," I replied. "I just wanted you to know that my apology was a part of an experiment I am making, an attempt to get my life straight. I think it is beginning to work."

He stopped in his tracks. He looked at me for a moment, and then asked if we could walk together. We walked round the quad perhaps twenty times, while he told me how lonely and despairing men like me had made him. "I have got nervous. I can't work properly. I've felt I must break out somehow." He seemed in the mood to do something quite desperate.

He decided that evening to make the same experiment that I was making. His change was obvious to everyone. Next term he got a first in his first examinations, followed by another in his finals. It was the first time in my life that I had really helped someone.

"You know, Garth," was his comment, "I could never have told you if you had not apologised to me that time."

Restitution is not just a clearing up of the past. It is a great stride into the future. Hundreds of marriages have been saved by it. This very day I had lunch with a couple who were to have signed their divorce papers. He is an army officer. His restitution brought them together two days ago. There is a glow of happiness and love in their eyes as they speak together, where three days ago there was hostility and the coldness of death. Many an industrial situation, many a national problem has been set on the road to solution by the same simple, costly act. "Honest apology," runs the song, "is the highroad to honest peace."

First be sure that the conviction of sin comes from God, and comes to the person himself. If it does, hold your friend firmly, though not heavily, to it.

One footnote about restitution. No one has the right to make restitution that implicates a third party. The Christian confesses his own sins, not those of other people.

* * * * * *

Another implication of decision is that you should make your new position known to your friends and family. Secret decisions seldom last.

As I walked back from Kit's room, I met my closest friend, whom we will call Jackman, in the college lodge. We were reading law and playing rugger together.

"Where have you been?" he asked. "I've been looking for you everywhere."

I knew this was a moment for truth. "I've been with Kit Prescott," I gulped. "I've made an experiment. I have asked God to take control of my life."

"You fool!" he said, and later brought round most of the Rugby XV to add their equally colourful expressions and persuasions. Nothing could have been better for me. My resolve was not very firm, but I was not going to be put off by a lot of toughs.

Putting Things Right

I am always grateful to God that he made my path with my friends so easy. I had to make no opportunities. They were made for me. Being straight at once with Jackman was my salvation. Everyone in college soon knew, and some came secretly to ask me about it.

The person who makes a secret decision is like the army recruit who tells his sergeant major that he would prefer not to parade or wear the uniform.

Chapter Ten
FOLLOW THROUGH

April has come to this Suffolk farm.

The winter wheat stands sea-green and bushy, tall enough to hide a hare. Barley and oats, sown a month since, press up in their ranks of lighter green like massed armies of fine spears. The miracle of rebirth, no man's doing, has come to us again.

The farmer and his workers have played their part. The land has been ploughed and harrowed, drilled and harrowed again. And the endless toil will go on, until finally the corn is harvested, and the plough turns up the stubbles once more. For though the miracle has happened and the corn is through the earth, there is never a time of rest. The farmer can never say: "Aha. My job is done. Now we will sleep till harvest." A keen eye must be kept cocked for pests, diseases and seeding thistles, while numberless other jobs are coming up each day.[1] The farmer who fails in this will lose his farm. The War Agricultural Committee will take it from him and give it to another.

Many Christians will applaud firm treatment for

---

[1] These farming methods are, of course, long outdated today, but the principle stands.

the sleepy farmer. Yet many of us expect a good spiritual harvest when we neglect as badly or worse the spiritual crops God gives us. We see them through the ground. We rejoice as our friend gives his life to God. Then we feel that our work is done, and we turn to other fields.

Pastures new are ever attractive. But that way leads to stunted harvests. To abandon the spiritual child as he embarks shakily on his new life is heartless and irresponsible. It is on a par with parents who, seeing their first-born pink and squalling in the nurse's arms, should remark, "Thank heavens that's over. Our work is complete. Let him bring himself up."

* * * * * *

Jesus saw his spiritual children in quite another light. During the three years of his ministry, he poured everything into twelve men.

How does he do it?

He asks them to live with him. He spends all of most days with them. He shares his triumphs with them – and his temptations. He "thrills with joy" when he sees his vision for them coming true. He is saddened, and starts again, when they are obstinate, competitive, of little faith. Every day and always, refusing to be tempted away to "swifter", more spectacular ways of world reform, he pours his life out into them, building them up individually and as a fighting force. At the end of his life he is able to report: "I kept those you had given me here in your

Following Through

name. I have watched over them and not one is lost except the one who chose to be lost and this was to fulfil the scriptures."[1]

And after his death? They become "the men who have turned the world upside down."[2]

What does Jesus do for these people? What does he do for them, which we too can do through his strength for those that come to us?

First, Jesus has a long, strong vision for Peter and his friends. He is not out to make them just a little better, slightly more respectable or more tolerant editions of their old selves. He is out to make them spiritual revolutionaries.

He calls them immediately after the Temptation. They are his answer to the specious world solutions that the devil proposed. They are his alternative programme. It may have been months before he could disclose to Peter the destiny that is in store for him. But it is in his mind for him from the beginning,[3] from the day he decided that a dedicated handful of people is the most enduring gift he can give the world.

We need the same long vision for those who come to us. Only in the gleam of such a view will we have the patience, and the courage to demand people to "sanctify themselves", in St Francis of Assisi's words, to the point where "society will be sancti-

[1] John 17:12
[2] Acts 17:6
[3] John 1:42–51

fied". In the light of a sufficient vision we dare not ask less.

"Have a ten years' vision for him," someone told me about a specially difficult person. Thank God that Kit and others had for me. Otherwise I should still be on the materialistic scrap-heap where they found me.

A ten years' vision is not easily obtained. It will mean hard thought, much study of the people concerned and more prayer. Often we Christians shirk it. That is why so many Christian communities, clubs, homes and even churches can be death-traps to the new revolutionary.

He comes to them, this spiritual child, with the flush of adventure upon him. Too often, if he is not ignored, he is given nothing more adventurous to aim at than that one day he may take the bag round in church or read the lesson. To such mediocrity do we reduce people who would, in the hands of a Francis, an Ignatius or a Wesley, be tempered into the swords of Christ.

Jesus gives Peter and his friends each new step as they are ready. He does not tell them everything he sees for them all at once.

Take Peter. He calls him in words chosen to capture a fisherman's heart: "I will make you a fisher of men."[1]

Not till months later, at Caesarea Philippi, does he

---

[1] Matthew 4:19

Following Through

tell him his destiny – that he will be the girder, the linchpin of the growing world fellowship.[1]

Soon afterwards, he hints at more to come. "I have many things to tell you, but you cannot bear them now."[2]

But it is not until after Peter's balloon of self-assurance has been finally punctured by his betrayal that he can give him his final commission – "Feed my sheep" – and tell him to what extremities of suffering that destiny will lead him.[3]

When you take a ship into harbour you can seldom go direct to the berth that is prepared for her. You need to know the berth. But you must steer from light to light. Otherwise, you will hit the headlands and the wharfs that lie in the direct path. Your job is to spot each light – and steer for it purposefully.

Jesus built into Peter and the others, as he travelled and worked with them, the qualities they needed to match their destiny.

Jesus seems to have aimed at two great changes in Peter:

First, he is always trying to show Peter that spiritual growth in people is more important than success in his own work – to make him a living answer to materialism.

Thus he calls him to be a "fisher of men." And later, when Peter returns to fishing for fish, he seeks

---

[1] Matthew 16:17–18
[2] John 16:12
[3] John 21:18–19

him again and re-commissions him. Peter is grieved when Jesus asks three times: "Do you love me?" Why did Jesus ask? Because his criterion is, "If you love me, keep my commands."[1] Had he not told this fisher of fish to fish for men? And here he is back at the beginning again. Now he re-commissions him to the same task – to feed the lambs and care for the sheep.

Second, Jesus is always bringing Peter back to the challenge that he must be a wholly Spirit-led personality, one who can always be relied upon to seek God's thought before his own or other peoples'.

It happens on the way to Caesarea Philippi. For when does he first tell Peter of his high destiny? When he can say: "Blessed are you, Simon Bar-Jona! For flesh and blood has not revealed this to you, but my Father . . ."[2] And when does he turn and call Peter "Satan"? When he has to say to him: "Your thoughts are the thoughts of men, not the thoughts of God."[3] In the Garden, as they take him away, Peter generously but unguidedly strikes with his sword. Back Jesus pulls him to God's will: "The cup which my Father hath given me, shall I not drink it?"[4]

By the lakeside he is at Peter's self-will again: "When you were young, you girded yourself and walked where you would; but when you are old, you

[1] John 14:15
[2] Matthew 16:17
[3] Matthew 16:23
[4] John 18:11

Following Through 99

will stretch out your hands and another will gird you and carry you where you do not wish to go."[1]

And on the Joppa roof, as Cornelius' messengers, the forerunners of the Gentile world, approach, the same old battle takes place.[2]

It is the battle between Peter's ingrained religious point of view – the best he knows – and God's plan. On this issue depends whether the new understanding of God shall be cramped into a tiny country or made available for the world. Because Jesus has shown him the way through those other battles, he beats his old temptation now. Later, Paul has to remind him of it, when Peter comes to Antioch and only eats with the Jewish Christians.[3]

Jesus surely left us his dealings with Peter as a pattern and prototype. For this is the stature that the great Christians have sought down the ages – to become skilled changers of people and wholly God-directed personalities.

---

[1] John 21:18
[2] Acts 10
[3] Galatians 2:11–14

Chapter Eleven
GROWTH

How to help the spiritual child grow towards this stature?

Many take a gloomy view of this matter. On seeing a spiritual baby they mutter, with much shaking of the head and well within its hearing, "Dear me. It will never last." And here is the strangest fact of all. Such prophets of woe are often regarded as very wise, whereas anyone who made the same remark over a lusty and squalling physical infant would be considered an ass.

One reason for this difference is plain. Generations of physical parents have been far more determined than their spiritual prototypes that their children should "last". They have been willing to sacrifice leisure, comfort and possessions to make it possible. They have studied childrens' needs. They have worked out, and passed on from one generation to another, a way of life which gives children the maximum chance of flourishing.

What is that way? Its fundamentals are simple. They are three: food, air and exercise.

The spiritual child's requirements are just as simple. To grow to adulthood he too needs food, air and exercise.

FOOD is primarily the Bible. "Man shall not live by bread alone but by every word that proceeds from the mouth of God."[1] It is a sustaining diet, as Bunyan's Christian and millions like him have found on their golden perilous journey.

Now your friend may be well acquainted with the Bible. He may read it regularly, but feel that he misses the strength he could be getting out of it. On the other hand, he may be one of the modern millions who have either never read the Bible at all, or have long ago rejected it as dull or impractical. In either case, change will soon alter his attitude. He now possesses a key to this spiritual larder far more effective than all the commentaries in the world. For the Bible was written by people in action for people in action.

The Bible, by itself, has been the instrument of converting millions through the centuries – and still does today. I think of a worker who came to a centre some of us were living in to repair the air-raid shelter. He sensed the happiness about the place, and before a week was out, had cornered one of the inhabitants and given his life to God. Next day someone noticed a light in the shelter during the dinner hour. There was the labourer, forgetful of food and surroundings, reading the Bible. He had just finished Matthew. "Better than any novel" was his comment. His only disappointment was that Mark told the same story all over again.

---

[1] Deuteronomy 8:3; Matthew 4:4

Growth

There he found people very like himself setting out on the self-same path. From which, this is clear. If you want the Bible to live for you, start living out its truths yourself. Mark Twain used to say that it was not the parts of the Bible he did not understand that worried him, but the parts he understood only too well.

* * * * * *

AIR. A person must breathe in or suffocate; he must breathe out or burst. It is the same with prayer. It should be two-way. Many people do suffocate spiritually because they breathe out, but never breathe in. They are so busy telling God what to do for them that they never listen to what He wants them to do for Him. Two-way prayer is the kind practised by Christ himself, and by his disciples in the Acts of the Apostles. They expected their Father to tell them what to do.[1]

So be sure your spiritual child breathes in as well as out, that he gives regular and adequate time to let God speak to him. The best time to set aside is the first hour of the day.[2] Then he will be sure of starting right. And it is a discipline that most great Christians down the ages have found essential. Jesus himself went out into the hills to pray early in the morning.

[1] See *Listening to the God who Speaks* by Klaus Bockmuehl (Helmers and Howard, Colorado Springs, 1990)
[2] *An Introduction to the Devout Life*, St. Francis de Sales (Hodder and Stoughton), p.64

Wesley, even in his eighty-eighth year, got up at four for the purpose.

A quarter of an hour will be enough listening, probably, for a beginning. Then your friend can increase it as he feels the need. Things will conspire to make this listening difficult. For the Devil does not like people planning their days with God. But if your friend does it, and sticks to it, he will receive illumination on old problems and situations and creative thoughts about new ones. His life will become rich and purposeful. Thoughts will come which will lead to far-reaching changes in a home, a business, a school, an industry, a nation. Often too, like Noah, he will be "warned of God of things not seen as yet"[1] – a prescience sadly lacking in modern statesmanship.

Another time-honoured trick of the Devil is to try to make the time of listening vague and ineffective. He makes a man too proud to do what St. Augustine did, to write down the thoughts that God gives him.[2] The result? Concentration is poor. Everything floats through the mind like those ideas that jostle each other but never crystallise into thought, between sleeping and waking.

Why should we treat God with less respect than someone who dictates a telegram to us over the telephone? Why should we dismiss him as too impracticable to give us any thought worthy of writing down?

[1] Hebrews 11:7
[2] San Augustino, Soliloqui, ed. Antonio Manzella, 1572

John Donne called the prophets "God's secretaries".[1] The post is open to all who will pay the price. And God will give us ever greater commissions as we prove ourselves obedient.

The early morning quiet time is just the beginning of the God-directed day. Next you need to help your friend to refer each decision to God, simply, as it arises. So gradually a new, a guided personality is born.

I am lastingly grateful that, during the first days of my listening, Kit Prescott came and listened with me. This was a great help to me. For often doubts would attack me. And very often I would be uncertain whether some thought given to me was really God's guidance or not. Kit's longer experience and his loving determination not to let me off with a second best, were reassuring and bracing.

Indeed, here is a vital principle of this matter of listening. Whenever in doubt, check your own thoughts with someone else who has those qualities of love and firmness. There is a passage in "The Little Flowers of St. Francis", which illustrates this principle. Francis was in "agonizing doubt" whether to start public speaking or not. So, while he himself sought clarity, he sent messages to St. Clare and others of his friends asking them to do the same. Each and all received the same answer – and Francis set out on his triumphant journey.[2]

---

[1]Sermon preached at Denmark House on December 14, 1617, in presence of Queen Anne, consort of James I
[2]*Little Flowers*, Chapter 16

If your spiritual child gets colic, as all children do, the trouble may be one of many. It may be the indulgence of some old temptation, or a flirtation with some new one. But in nine times out of ten, whatever the immediate issue, the basic problem is some failure in these quiet times. He may have stopped having them, or cut them short, and so lost the healthful power that they bring. Or he may have disobeyed some thought he has already received, and so be unable to get any more until he does obey. The remedy is to start again, give God adequate time and full attention and to obey the thoughts that come.

* * * * * *

EXERCISE. Jesus often gave people something to do which resulted in their growth. He sent out seventy disciples two by two with exact instructions what to do – and rejoiced on their return.

At other times growth resulted, without instruction, from something he did with them. He invited himself to lunch with Zacchaeus, and soon Zacchaeus was declaring to everyone the restitutions he felt led to make.

He cured a blind man in John 9 – and it led inevitably to the challenging of all Jerusalem. His neighbours naturally wanted to know what had happened to him. He told them the simple facts. It only took him some 34 words. The Pharisees, too, wanted to hear about it. He repeated his story – in 16 words this time. This exasperated them. They tried every dodge to shake him. They enlisted his parents against him, reminded him he was ill-educated, denounced the man who helped him as a blasphemer. They tried the Devil's splitting tactics, veiled with the pious "Give God the praise." To all this he simply replied: "I don't know about that; one thing I do know, that once I was blind and now I can see."

The point is that he spoke up to, never beyond, his experience. He stuck to that experience, which no-one could gainsay, and refused to argue.

Note how the clash of action develops him. At the beginning he is just a joyful man relating his good fortune. But as he tells his tale again and again, his confidence grows. He is learning to articulate his message. Then the learned men harangue him, and finally ask him what he thinks of Jesus. By now he can say: "I think he is a prophet". They lose their tempers. How cool he becomes. He takes the offensive in stout, shrewd manner. By the time Jesus visits him again – and it is worth noting that Jesus does revisit him – he has got through to the real truth about him and is ready to give himself wholly to his purposes.

Exercise develops spiritual muscles as nothing else can. I had the same experience with my crowd at college as the ex-blind man had with his in Jerusalem. The fact that I met Jackman in the Lodge on my way back from Kit's digs on the day of my decision and that, later that night, I was visited by a dozen of the college rugger side put me on my mettle. They did for me what Cortes did for his tiny force landing in Mexico – they burnt my boats behind me. And there were times for me, as there were for his desperate band, when the lack of means of retreat was my greatest safety.

Action is helpful too, because it provides the experience which a beginner needs to combat the doubts natural to his condition. Many a time Kit would come in and find me in the gloom of doubt. "Had I been a fool to do it? Was there a God anyway?" He knew it was temptation and sometimes he would tell me so and help me to see the position straight. But very often he would do nothing of the sort. He would not discuss my difficulties. He would simply carry me off to tell someone about the things which *had* happened to me. As I did so, as I got out of myself and thought of someone else's needs, perspective would return and with it the sense of divine grace and commissioning. When back in my rooms I surveyed the old doubt, it would look so silly that I could laugh at it.

Here is the wisdom of Böhler's advice to Wesley. On a day of crisis, John Wesley asked Peter Böhler ("by whom, in the hand of the great God, I was, this Sunday, the fifth, clearly convinced of unbelief, of the want of that faith whereby alone we are saved")[1] whether he should stop preaching. "By no means," answered Böhler. "Preach faith till you have it; then,

---

[1] John Wesley's Journal, March 4 1738

Growth 109

because you have it, you will preach faith."[1] It was that action which sustained Wesley till he came twelve weeks later to the room in Aldersgate Street where his heart was "strangely warmed".[2] Peter Böhler spent much of those intervening weeks with Wesley. He stood by him as Jesus stood by the blind man. And it is easy to see from the Journal what a thirst Wesley had for his company. Wesley preached faith. It was the faith he saw in his friend and in those to whom Böhler introduced him.

Böhler took him into action. More particularly he set him to work on his brother Charles. The immediate result? "My brother was very angry and told me I did not know what mischief I had done by talking thus.[3] And, indeed, (interpolates Wesley fifty years later) it did please God then to kindle a fire which I trust shall never be extinguished." Böhler, meanwhile, was planning to embark for Carolina. But he did not go until Charles too had been "convinced"[4] and the two brothers could march forward to their destiny together.

Very often it is helpful thus to go into action with people who are making a new start. They are sure to meet snags, and some of them will be with people from whom they might expect the most support. The Pharisees enlisted the ex-blind man's parents against him. During their struggle for the faith which Böhler

[1] Ibid, March 4, 1738
[2] Ibid May 24, 1738
[3] Ibid, April 23, 1738
[4] Charles Wesley's Journal, May 21, 1738

offered them, John Wesley had his earliest opposition from his best loved brother, though oddly enough it was Charles, not John, who broke through first to the faith and freedom which enabled them to change so much in the Britain of their day.[1]

---

[1] *John Wesley, Anglican*, pp 31–2; *Strangely Warmed*, pp 39–41

Chapter Twelve
FAMILIES

Naturally, it is the person's family or closest friends who are most sensitive when someone gives God control of his life. Often they are delighted, and decide to take the new path themselves. I think of one family where the father and mother, five brothers or sisters and numerous cousins did so, when the most unlikely of them all, the eldest daughter, became different. Often, again, relatives are more cautious for the best of reasons. They want to be sure that the person concerned is not taking a step which will be regretted. They try him or her out, watching to see whether the change is genuine and whether it is the person's own deepest conviction or something he or she has adopted under the pressure of someone else.

On other occasions one or more relatives may be immediately antagonistic. Sometimes this is because they feel an attempt to live a life of faith is impossible, or, at least, something they are unwilling to try for themselves. Or they may resent the fact that, where they had been the most important people in a person's life till then, someone else – God or what the person thinks is God – has usurped their place. The stronger the family bond has been, the more likely is this last concern to be important.

Jesus himself had difficulty, at least once with his family. When he was speaking to a large hostile crowd, his family asked to speak with him, with the idea of restraining him. His comment was, "Who are my mother and my brothers?", and then, pointing to his disciples he added, "Here are my mother and my brothers! Whoever does the will of God is my brother, and sister and mother."[1]

This "hard saying", which many find difficult to understand, did not mean that Jesus loved his family any less than before. He was simply saying that God and those who obeyed God must come first in his life. Surely it means for us that we should never be deflected from obeying what we are sure is God's will for us by anything our families and friends may say or think or demand. Remember that Jesus' mother and brothers were all united with the Eleven after the Ascension and through Pentecost,[2] and his brother, James, became head of the church in Jerusalem.

We, of course, are not to be compared with Jesus. We often make mistakes. But, for us, it is clear that any appeasement because of what our families may think is wrong. Often it is not what they really want. In their inner hearts families are disappointed if we sacrifice principle for fear of displeasing them. Also,

---

[1] Matthew 12:46–50
[2] Acts 1:14

we might be closing the door for them, against the time when one or other of them may feel they themselves are in need of something deeper.

The most common mistake with families is to try and rush them into your way of life. Because they are dear to you, because you so ardently wish them to have the new joy which you have found – you are apt to jettison the stage of trust-winning and charge in bald-headed.

In my own case I was particularly clumsy with one of my brothers, the one I loved most. He was nearly five years older than I yet, throughout my childhood, he played all kinds of games with me, which must have been very boring for him. When I was ten, my father died, and it was this brother who did most to fill his place. By the time I made my experiment, he was an agnostic, and insecure about where his future lay, and I did not understand how much our relationship meant to him. I went in far too baldly, introduced him to just the wrong people and expected him to be as interested as I was in what I was finding. It was only several years later, when he asked me to be the best man at his wedding, that I knew I had managed to rebuild some part of the confidence between us.[1]

---

[1] Even forty years later, when I visited him with my daughter, he brought up again how much I had hurt him with some bitterness. On my last visit before he died, I tried to tell him how grateful I was for all he had done for me. You can imagine my joy when he put his hand on mine and said, "You've been a wonderful brother, a wonderful brother."

The fact is that there is no place where the trust stage is more important than at home. Make restitution humbly for any way in which you have wronged any of your family, and if they ask questions, tell them simply what you are trying to do. But don't become a bore and speak of nothing else. Just live the new life you have found unobtrusively, and show that you love them more, not less, than before.

Chapter Thirteen
THREE LEVELS OF LIFE

The process of continued change may be described in this way: there are three levels on which a person can live – the level of desire, the level of duty, and the level of grace. Spiritual progress in a person, a home or a nation is moving from levels one and two up to the glorious freedom of the grace of God.

We all know the level of desire, for we have all existed there for longer or shorter periods. It is the dominion of sheer instinct, where "I want" is supreme. Spinoza wrote of it in a famous passage: "The things that are esteemed among men as the highest good (as is witnessed by their works) can be reduced to three, Riches, Fame and Lust: and by these the mind is so distracted that it can scarcely think of any other good." In fact it is a state of tyranny, and like every tyranny conceals a bitter end beneath a sugary surface. "The mind is so absorbed," the philosopher continues, "as if it had attained rest in some good; this hinders it from thinking of anything else. But after fruition a great sadness follows which, if it does not absorb the mind, will yet disturb and blunt it."

The level of duty – "I ought" – is many people's highest ideal. In some societies at different periods, it has reached a fine standard of tradition. Yet it is sub-Christian. And it can quickly degenerate into a tyranny where the good forbids the best.

Much of modern Christianity is duty-bound. That is why it sometimes looks cold, sterile and unattractive to those it should be winning, the dwellers in desire. They ignore duty-driven religion as dull and long-faced. And you can understand it. For "the glorious liberty of the sons of God" does not come on this level. There is nothing here which outlives, outloves and outlaughs the pagan world.

Duty brings its own sins with it. One is self-importance – when the "I" becomes more important than the "ought". Another is self-righteousness. A third is man-pleasing, for the duty swiftly becomes a matter of doing what someone about you or some crowd of people expect of you. The Christian who does not rise above this level is ever in danger of back-sliding. For it takes a passion to cure a passion, and no permanent cure for the full-blooded demands of the flesh can be found in this dim region.

What is the level of grace? You will know it if you have ever, however briefly, lived upon it, or seen someone else do so. The great Christians down the ages experienced it and wrote of it. Brother Lawrence had it in the rush and clamour of his kitchen. Francis knew its sweetness as he trudged the roads and set men's hearts aflame. Paul drank deep of it – and described it in his epistles, distinguishing it from the law or duty. Thomas à Kempis, in *The Imitation of*

Three Levels of Life

Christ, marvellously points the contrast between it and nature or desire.

Grace is the free gift of God. It cannot be earned or bought. But God has no favourites. He will give it to all who want it enough, to all who are willing to pay the price of living above the levels of desire and duty.

Grace is the place where your longing, duty and action harmonise. It gives you the freedom where, with St. Augustine, you increasingly "love God and do as you please". It includes everything that is good in the level of duty – for in God's plan no real duties conflict.

Here is realised the truth – "Whose service is perfect freedom." The secret is God's direction sought in each detail and obeyed with His help.

It is this level of grace to which we must all aim ourselves and to which we must help our friends to aspire.

First, it will mean clearing the jungle of desire, area by area perhaps, as the Spirit brings them to light. Spinoza's three must be tackled for no one can be free who is the slave of the desire for Riches, Fame or Lust. It will come by degrees. Jesus said to His disciples that He had many things to tell them which they could not bear at the moment. And He promised that the Spirit would lead them into all truth. So, as we can bear it, day by day, step by step, the Spirit turns His searchlight on some habit or indulgence, some pride or self-will, and demands that it should be eradicated.

Sometimes the dealing with such an area – the rooting out of some long-established habit of thought or action perhaps – is a prolonged fight. For the period of the battle the strife is very sharp. The sin which you had become so used to committing that you have ignored its presence and underestimated or even denied its force – that sin becomes horridly apparent at each minute of the day. Where formerly you were irritable and never noticed it, now you are brought up short many times a day as you find yourself being so. Where once impure thoughts and glances were accepted as normal, now as the Spirit spotlights each occasion, you see how much of your life was made up of such things. You stub your toe on them every step you take. You say to yourself: "If I go on fighting this thing, letting nothing unwillingly pass, I shall do nothing else all my life." And the temptation is to give up the unequal struggle. That is the very point when salvation is near. If you resist this last Devil's trick, victory will come. The tempter will be off and, very literally, "angels come and minister unto you".

The life-changer's part, when a friend is fighting such battles, is first of all to be quite sure that he is fighting his own battles himself. I think with shame of those I have failed at such times because I myself have slackened my warfare – or am refusing to face some revealed next step. The other fellow senses it at once, and knows you are no use to him in his need.

Now, as always, the other task is to be aware of

what is happening in your friend. Again and again it is written of St. Francis that he "knew in the Spirit what was going on in his friend's and friar's hearts." To one who was going through a prolonged agony of temptation many miles away, he sent two brothers to say that he "loved him singularly". He called to him another, who was harbouring secret and venomous thoughts and so cured him. As the old chronicler writes, "As our Lord Jesus Christ says in the Gospel: 'I know my sheep and they know me', so the blessed Father St. Francis, as a good shepherd, knew by divine revelation all the merits and virtues of his companions; and so he knew their defects, for which reason he knew how to apply the best remedy for each."[1]

We lesser people must learn to do the same for each other. And, through God's power, we are able. We can be near at the hour of need with the assurance that "He will not allow us to be tempted beyond what we are able."[2]

---

[1] *Little Flowers*, chapters 31, 38; *The Mirror of Perfection*, chapter 106
[2] 1 Corinthians 10:13

Chapter Fourteen
BUILDING A TEAM

Al Capone, for a decade King of the Chicago underworld, was talking one day to a "decent citizen". They were canvassing frankly gangsterdom's hope of survival. "You decent guys," said Capone finally, "are 99% of the population. But you will never get rid of us. You can't unite."

In the years between the wars other greater men worked on the same principle. Hitler banked on it in his fight with the German democratic parties – and won out. He tried it again with the European democracies – and swallowed them one by one.

Unity. Yes, that is the secret of strength. The future belongs to the people who are united by their common commitment. The cohesion of the materialists is assured. Their action is controlled by the very laws of life. All those on the get – whether organised into 'isms' or just self-seeking individuals – will play into each other's hands. Even if they fight each other for power, they can between them bring the world to chaos – just as two dogs fighting in a china shop will not improve the crockery, even if one is killed.

And what of the forces of faith? What do they oppose to this militant alliance of the materialists?

Have we nothing better than the divided and ineffective front that Capone and Hitler banked upon?

Often, alas, we have not. Yet we can have. All down history there have been times when fighting forces have arisen to turn back the trends of the age. Often the band of fighters has been quite small. Humanly their chances have been poor. Yet through their tremendous unity and complete abandon of self they have been formidable beyond all expectation. We must always remember that, as Florence Allshorn said, "Whether the thing looks possible or impossible is really not your question. You have your task in it, but you will be beaten by it if you let go faith in the fact that God also has his task in it. He will bring about the issue, not you."[1]

What are the principles of fighting unity?

1. *Live in the Light*. The sentence of condemnation was, according to St. John, that Light had come into the world and yet men preferred darkness to light. In Chapter 3:20–21 he goes on: "It is because their actions have been evil: for anyone whose practices are corrupt loathes the light and will not come out into it, in case his actions are exposed, whereas anyone whose life is true comes out in the light, to make it plain that his actions have been divinely prompted."

Teamwork depends on the people who work together knowing each other through and through. How can we develop and use each other fully if we

---

[1] Quoted in *A New Day* by Dorothy Prescott (Blandford) p 221

do not know each others' deepest needs and strengths and fears and longings? Nothing breaks fellowship and effective unity so quickly and decisively as temptations indulged or suppressed, but undefeated, or little criticisms and jealousies not confessed and quit. With such it is impossible to get what Wellington called "an unanimous army".

Frank Buchman worked out this age-old principle anew for himself and his work when with one of his earliest teams in China. One of his companions describes it: "We found that two of us would sometimes get together and secretly vent something we disliked about another. To end that kind of thing we decided we would share with the person concerned rather than with another the dislike we felt. Then not only did we share our own faults whenever they stuck their heads up, but we sought guidance to end our quarrels and cement the team into the ideal fellowship."

St. James evidently had a similar experience. His recipe for teamwork was: "Confess your sins one to another and pray for one another, that you may be healed; the prayers of the righteous have a powerful effect."[1]

2. *All take orders – from God*. This is inspired democracy. In this spirit divergent views enrich instead of causing division. In a cabinet, a board meeting or a church where all are keener on what's right than who's right, each builds into the whole. The joint

---
[1] James 5:16

conception grows. The common mind, with God the arbiter and inspirer, brings forth a greater plan than individuals or groups of individualists could produce.

* * * * * *

Teamwork is one thing. Team-building is another.

Teamwork starts when I get beyond the attitude: "I know best, keep your hands off." It involves the heart-belief that I can't do as well alone as with a team. Pretty obvious, you say? Yes, indeed. I too can see how necessary a team is – to almost everyone else. Why, it keeps them up to the mark, balances their judgement, applies goad or rein as needed and enriches parched life and limited powers with infinite joy and variety. Yet it is remarkable, when it is I myself that am involved, how often I feel deep down that if only people would leave me alone the job would get done quicker and better. For it is costly to accept the mind of others on everything I do and think. It means the pain of an enlarging vision – a process most necessary of all, funnily enough, in the fields where I think myself strongest. For there I am most often blind to the new riches God has in store.

Yes, teamwork can be costly. But team-building is more so. It calls for great qualities of heart and head. It means thinking of each task not simply in terms of getting it done, – which is important, yet may by itself just be materialism in a subtle form – but rather in terms of human beings: whom to do it with or through, who will be developed by the adventure or responsibility. It means clothing every plan with people and putting people first. Its great enemies are the self-importance that pleads that you alone can do it, and the materialism that makes things more important than people.

I think of the way Peter Howard and his wife, Doë, went about things on his farm, after they had given their lives to God. They decided that "in every farm decision, as in every other decision of our lives, we would do our utmost to find God's will and to carry it through".

The first battle was for teamwork. Peter had been accustomed to say what he wanted done – and to hell with the other fellow. But his thought now was to make the whole staff a team. It was sometimes a struggle to accept ideas from the old farm hands, and even from war-time land-girls fresh from town jobs. But he won that battle. And soon the neighbouring farmers who had prophesied disaster for this daring townsman saw that he had succeeded. Output went up 100%. The near-derelict farm was officially rated Grade A by the War Agricultural Committee.

But that was only part. He began to think of the farm not just as an industrial concern – and anyone who has lived upon one knows that a farm is that – but as a means of developing character. He used it for team-building.

What did this involve? It meant living in the belief that if the spiritual needs of every member of the staff were met, the farm work would prosper as a by-product. It meant resolutely going out to meet those needs.

You only need a little experience of the land to realise that there is an urgent job for every minute of every day in the year on a farm. I once asked Peter "Don't you ever get impatient when there's a rush job on?"

"Yes, sometimes," he replied, "but when we put the job before the person it always goes wrong. When the person is put first and every failure is used not to bring fear to him but to bring any needed change or development to the individual concerned, then the jobs get done in record speed." Old farm hands were astonished.

* * * * * *

"It is better to put ten men to work than to do ten men's work." So many people, especially spiritual leaders, do not believe this. So their work is circumscribed by their own limited energies. As they grow older, it declines. Many of them just have nervous breakdowns.

Buchman has set his face against this individualistic course. His chief delight is to get other people doing things which they never dreamt they could do. The ordinary person, plus God, says he, can do the extraordinary thing.

If someone comes to him with a bright idea, it is ten to one that he will answer, "Fine. You do it." So the person who has thought his suggestion out is

Building a Team

encouraged, not repressed. And the person who has brought forward a half-baked scheme, hoping he will get Buchman to execute it for him, is sent back to think again.

But though Buchman delegates jobs, he does not slip out of the responsibility. He conceives it his task to see that the person to whom he has delegated it is in top spiritual form.

I remember once being with him at an assembly where the audiences totalled 25,000 people. They had come in 21 special trains from all over Britain. A party of 500 had arrived from Holland alone. And with them came the press and the news reels. I was in charge of the press arrangements.

I was just twenty-five years old at the time and had only recently joined Buchman's international team. Yet he had encouraged me throughout the campaign and never shown any qualm at entrusting me with this vital post where a careless word could mar his work.

Then one night I was sitting up late, writing a report for a weekly paper. Buchman came in and began to help me. By this time I had become self-confident, and began to think that I knew best. I told him and many others that they had better leave me alone and let me get on with it.

Next morning before breakfast I was listening to God. I felt shame at my attitude of the night before. I went in to Buchman's room to tell him so. He also had been reflecting. He had written down: "Garth: the piggishness of possessiveness." And it was underlined three times. He went on to amplify it – definitely, incisively, devastatingly. And he would not go on to the planning of a momentous day until he had straightened me out. Thousands of people would be waiting for his message at ten o'clock. Yet he spent half his time of listening that morning thinking of me. He knew it was useless to change the crowd if he did not change me first.

And he did not assume that the change was effected in a day. With humour and relentless resolve he pursued me until the day in America six months later when he suddenly said: "You know, Garth – that possessiveness of yours has quite gone." I think he was even then being over-charitable, for there have been recurrences, but at least since then I recognise the disease when I get it, and know there is an answer.

"Do big things together." That is a principle which wins wars. It will be equally important when peace comes. The massed forces of materialism will not be beaten any other way.

Chapter Fifteen

YOUR MAJOR PASSION

When I was ten I read that you could buy at the chemist's shop, for the moderate sum of five shillings, all the physical elements of a man.

The idea intrigued me. I borrowed the necessary cash and set off to the chemist. An hour later I was sitting on the edge of my bed gazing at my row of little bottles.

Whom should I make? The Archbishop of Canterbury? My favourite aunt? Or Pat Hendren, my current cricketing hero?

It was then that I hit the snag. Someone pointed out that I lacked an important ingredient. In none of my bottles was the element called Life. It was a deathblow to my venture. I turned from my bottles in disgust. There they stood gathering dust for many a day.

This child-time misadventure springs to mind when I hear certain people discussing the business of changing human nature. These folk seem to feel that it is just a matter of discovering the knack of it, of finding and following the right technique. They quite forget that changing human nature means giving new life, and that the gift cannot be bought or wangled or manipulated from person to person.

The power to help people is the gift of God on each occasion. We do not change them. He changes them – often in spite of us, generally independent of us – yet sometimes through us. The amazing fact is that He is willing, even eager, to use us, that He will include us in His own task of creation.

The one condition is that we must be ready to pay the price of this partnership. We must change, if we wish to help others. For we cannot pass on what we have not got. Christianity, like the measles, is generally caught, rather than taught.

In fact we shall not only have to change once, but to change continually. Otherwise we will suffer the fate of the man in the story. This fellow had a religious experience in youth which he wrote down and stored in the attic. When people came to the house he used to fetch it down and read it to them. It got old and yellowed, and fell into disuse, for all his friends had heard it and everyone knew that he quarrelled with his wife. One day, however, a stranger called and he sent his wife for the paper. After much rummaging she returned. "My dear," she said, "I fear that the mice have eaten your religious experience."

"They must upward still and onward who would keep abreast of truth." People instinctively know whether we are victorious in our own lives here and now. If we are, they will come to us. If we are not, no amount of technical knowledge will fill the gap. Canon Mackay says of the Franciscans, "They treated their persecutions as a comical and delightful adven-

Your Major Passion

ture and it was, of course, this spirit of theirs and not the things that Francis said which made converts – they themselves were their message."

We too must be our own message. We must live a life which attracts those we meet. And this is more than ever true today. People are hungry for spiritual truth. But they are God-shy. They seldom go to church, are weary of sermons and rarely read the Bible. They look for truth, demonstrated in people's lives.

We have to live a quality of life. It has to contain a fresh, spontaneous love for each person we meet – so that each feels, and is, the most important person on earth to us as we talk together. People – their growth to their full stature – must be our major passion. We must be ready to sacrifice anything for that. It will require that – and some. As St. Paul wrote to Timothy, "No soldier gets entangled in civil pursuits: his aim is to satisfy his commander."[1] That applies whatever job we are in.

John Wesley, in his endless, arduous journeyings, ever showed this passion for souls. It was his practice to speak to everyone he met on the deep questions of the human heart. Once, however, he made the experiment of not doing so on a coach journey from London to Leicester. Here is the entry about it in his Journal:

"For these two days I had made an experiment which I had so often and earnestly been pressed to

---

[1] 2 Timothy 2:4

do – speaking to none concerning the things of God unless my heart was free for it. And what was the event? Why, 1. That I spoke to none at all for fourscore miles together; no, not even to him that travelled with me in the chaise, unless a few words at the first setting out. 2. That I had no cross to bear or to take up, and commonly in an hour or two fell fast asleep. 3. That I had much respect shown me wherever I came; everyone behaving to me as a civil, good-natured gentleman. Oh, how pleasing is all this to flesh and blood. Need ye 'compass sea and land' to make 'proselytes' to this?"

Wesley never tried that experiment again.

My own attitude has often been, "Why risk a snub?" Yet time and again, when I have dared to do it, I have found that God has prepared the way.

Philip must have felt the edge of such temptations when he was ordered to take the desert road to Gaza and then, so to say, to mount the running board of the Rolls Royce which carried the Finance Minister of a foreign power. But when he obeyed, he found that official reading not the latest smutty verses from Rome, but passages of Isaiah which called aloud for Philip's experience to explain them. That day a life was changed.

So how to learn how to become a life-changer? The Duke of Wellington, asked how to become a great general, answered, "By fighting, sir, and plenty of it."

The best way to learn to change lives is by life-changing – and plenty of it.

Epilogue
1990

My first reaction on rereading this account of my experiences from fifty-five to forty-five years ago has been to see how many opportunities I have missed since then and how often I have frustrated God's will through disobedience, laziness or fears. At the same time, it is encouraging to see the people who have themselves become fishers of men and reshapers of events around them. I am grateful to God that he still sends me people and uses me to help them, as well as sending people who help me.

In 1946, three years after I completed this book, the long wished-for marriage with Margot took place. The years of waiting had often been painful, but had matured us both. We did not feel that they had been wasted, but thanked God when he gave us the green light to go ahead. He has already given us over forty happy and adventurous years together and taken us into many countries and the most varied situations. Naturally marriage increased the number of people who have come to us for help, and we remember the times when we have been used to bring an original or a deeper faith to other couples among our most satisfying experiences.

Another great joy has been to have two children,

now grown up, who chose early in life to accept God as their guide and who have continued in that faith in all aspects of their lives. They have also given us much. They have encouraged us when we felt down and also helped us to see and overcome our faults. With their help and Margot's, I am gradually learning to accept my age and to trust God and the Holy Spirit rather than my own activism.

I have no excuse for ever failing to do so. For, again and again, I have been privileged to see God work modern miracles not only in individuals, but, through them, in social, national and international affairs. Of these wider matters, I have written in other books, which are listed opposite the title page of this book. They describe, amongst other things, the significant part which men of faith have played in bringing countries together after generations of hatred, in assisting certain countries in Africa and elsewhere to freedom without bloodshed and in easing many social problems.

These changes, most of which I have observed personally, are, of course, only a tiny part of what the Holy Spirit is doing in our world. Indeed, the events of which I have written, whether contemporary or in past history, have only partly been brought about through the change in people, however essential that element has been. William Wilberforce and his co-workers, for example, could not have done what they did to suppress the slave trade and alter manners in England without their character changes and persistent teamwork. Equally, they would have failed if the Holy Spirit had not prepared the way and intervened in many ways.

Today we live in a world where universal norms of morality are no longer acknowledged, let alone practised. Meanwhile it is at last being widely recognised that the whole world must work together if it is to avoid environmental catastrophe. As I write, remarkable changes are taking place in Eastern Europe and elsewhere which could, theoretically, make global co-operation easier to achieve.

Whether these sudden changes will, in fact, lead to a better co-operation or only to anarchy and the multiplication of conflict will depend on the way peoples and their leaders in every country, not least in the West, decide to live. We need to get into the jet-stream of the Spirit, personally and nationally. It is hoped that readers of this little book may have found hints, at least, about how this can be done.